DATE DUE		

**BIO
HOLIDAY**

33577000654721
Greene, Meg.

Billie Holiday : a
biography

BILLIE HOLIDAY

Recent Titles in Greenwood Biographies

Jane Goodall: A Biography
Meg Greene

The Leakeys: A Biography
Mary Bowman-Kruhm

Arthur Ashe: A Biography
Richard Steins

Cesar Chavez: A Biography
Roger Bruns

F. Scott Fitzgerald: A Biography
Edward J. Rielly

Saddam Hussein: A Biography
Shiva Balaghi

Tiger Woods: A Biography
Lawrence J. Londino

Mohandas K. Gandhi: A Biography
Patricia Cronin Marcello

Muhammad Ali: A Biography
Anthony O. Edmonds

Martin Luther King, Jr.: A Biography
Roger Bruns

Wilma Rudolph: A Biography
Maureen M. Smith

Condoleezza Rice: A Biography
Jacqueline Edmondson

Arnold Schwarzenegger: A Biography
Louise Krasniewicz and Michael Blitz

BILLIE HOLIDAY

A Biography

By Meg Greene

GREENWOOD BIOGRAPHIES

GREENWOOD PRESS
WESTPORT, CONNECTICUT • LONDON

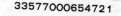

Library of Congress Cataloging-in-Publication Data

Greene, Meg.
   Billie Holiday: a biography / By Meg Greene.
      p. cm.—(Greenwood biographies)
   Includes bibliographical references and index.
   ISBN 0–313–33629–6 (alk. paper)
   1. Holiday, Billie, 1915–1959. 2. Singers—United States—Biography. I. Title.
   ML420.H58G68   2007
   782.42165092—dc22
   [B]   2006025382

British Library Cataloguing in Publication Data is available.

Library of Congress Catalog Card Number: 2006025382

ISBN 13: 978–0–313–33629–4
ISBN 10: 0–313–33629–6
ISSN: 1540–1900

First published in 2007

Greenwood Press, 88 Post Road West, Westport, CT 06881
An imprint of Greenwood Publishing Group, Inc.
www.greenwood.com

Printed in the United States of America

(∞)™

The paper used in this book complies with the
Permanent Paper Standard issued by the National
Information Standards Organization (Z39.48–1984).

10 9 8 7 6 5 4 3 2 1

CONTENTS

Series Foreword   vii

Introduction   ix

Timeline: Events in the Life of Billie Holiday   xiii

Chapter 1. Eleanora   1

Chapter 2. Billie   13

Chapter 3. Ladies and Gentlemen ... Billie Holiday   23

Chapter 4. A Rising Star   33

Chapter 5. On the Road   43

Chapter 6. "Strange Fruit"   55

Chapter 7. Life as Billie Holiday   65

Chapter 8. A Slow Descent into Hell   75

Chapter 9. Jazz's Falling Star   85

Chapter 10. The Spotlight Dims   97

Bibliography   111

Index   115

Photo essay follows page 54

SERIES FOREWORD

In response to high school and public library needs, Greenwood developed this distinguished series of full-length biographies specifically for student use. Prepared by field experts and professionals, these engaging biographies are tailored for high school students who need challenging yet accessible biographies. Ideal for secondary school assignments, the length, format, and subject areas are designed to meet educators' requirements and students' interests.

Greenwood offers an extensive selection of biographies spanning all curriculum-related subject areas including social studies, the sciences, literature and the arts, history and politics, as well as popular culture, covering public figures and famous personalities from all time periods and backgrounds, both historic and contemporary, who have made an impact on American and/or world culture. Greenwood biographies were chosen based on comprehensive feedback from librarians and educators. Consideration was given to both curriculum relevance and inherent interest. The result is an intriguing mix of the well-known and the unexpected, the saints and sinners from long-ago history and contemporary pop culture. Readers will find a wide array of subject choices from fascinating crime figures like Al Capone to inspiring pioneers like Margaret Mead, from the greatest minds of our time like Stephen Hawking to the most amazing success stories of our day like J. K. Rowling.

Although the emphasis is on fact, not glorification, the books are meant to be fun to read. Each volume provides in-depth information about the subject's life from birth through childhood, the teen years, and adulthood. A thorough account relates family background and education, traces personal and professional influences, and explores struggles, accomplishments, and contributions. A timeline highlights the most significant life events against a historical perspective. Bibliographies supplement the reference value of each volume.

INTRODUCTION

Legends are made, not born. Sometimes they are forgotten and disappear, fade away and die. Sometimes, though, they are larger than death and grow still larger after the subjects are gone, especially if death has taken them too violently and too soon. The music world is filled with such larger-than-life figures: Elvis Presley, John Lennon, Jim Morrison, Janis Joplin, Jimi Hendrix, and the blues singer Robert Johnson come immediately to mind. Their lives and their music were so intertwined that it becomes impossible to separate the music from the personality. It was that way with Billie Holiday. Dead for nearly a half century, Billie Holiday haunts us still. We can see her face, the dark eyes shining, the white gardenias bound in her hair. We can hear her voice, and sometimes, we can almost feel her presence.

Billie Holiday, or "Lady Day" as she was known, is the iconic female jazz singer. She has the timeless quality of a legend. Why? What has made her persona and her music so enduring? What has made her so dear to so many? Perhaps it is the mystery and the complexity of her life that continues to fascinate, for she is a study in contrasts. She was both sophisticated and unrefined, both guilty and innocent. Her voice is familiar, yet elusive. She was one of a kind, unique and inimitable. No one sounds like Billie Holiday; no one can.

As a singer, and no doubt as a woman, Billie Holiday was at once intimate and aloof. Her love songs express basic, even primal, emotions. Her versions of such standards as "You Go to My Head," "The Very Thought of You," "The Man I Love," and "Until the Real Thing Comes Along" convey the bewilderment, vulnerability, and yearning that come

with falling in love. Yet, no jazz singer has ever captured more fully the de-
vouring sense of loneliness and loss, as she did, for example, in her haunting renditions of "I Cover the Waterfront" or "I'll Be Seeing You." A tone
of melancholy longing and resignation finds its way into even some of her
more upbeat and joyful tunes, such as "What a Little Moonlight Can Do,"
"All of Me," or "Me, Myself, and I." This mixture of happiness and sadness,
she suggested, is the common lot of humanity.

Her life did not consist of equal parts; in her four decades, she knew
more sadness and tragedy than joy or love. As other writers have pointed
out, however, if not for the sorrow, there would be no legend, and if not
for the suffering, there would be no sainthood. The legend and the saint
are inseparable.

Yet, there is more to Billie Holiday than myth and legend. Her
contributions to jazz are real and tangible. Holiday transformed the art of
jazz singing, and it is no exaggeration to say that modern jazz singing began
with her. Before she appeared on the scene, jazz singers rarely personalized
their tunes. Only blues singers, such as Ma Rainey, Bessie Smith, and Dinah
Washington, did not sound generic and interchangeable. Bored by the popular songs that she had to sing and record early in her career, Holiday experimented by altering both the rhythm and the melody. She phrased behind
the beat and added harmonies derived from her favorite horn players, such
as Louis Armstrong and Lester Young. The results were often magical.

Jazz musicians speak through their instruments. Holiday's genius as a
vocalist lay in how she used her voice. She phrased her vocals like an
instrumentalist and was as much a musician as any of her accompanists.
"I don't think I'm singing," she once reflected. "I try to improvise like Les
Young, like Louis Armstrong, or someone else I admire. What comes out
is what I feel. I hate straight singing. I have to change a tune to my own
way of doing it. That's all I know."[1]

Not only was she the first to make an instrument of her voice, but she
was also the first to sense that technology had changed musical performance. Perhaps instinctively, she understood that the microphone made
possible a new style of singing. Technology can sometimes enhance human
qualities and extend human purposes, and so it was with Billie Holiday.
The microphone humanized her voice, enabling her to develop the ex-
pressive style for which she became famous. Without the microphone, the
sensitive, emotional nuances of her voice would have remained inaudible
and been lost.

According to Robert O'Meally, one of the many Holiday biographers,
Holiday's life and career is divided into three periods.[2] The first phase brought

the emergence of Holiday's distinctive singing style during the 1930s. The second phase began with her recording of "Strange Fruit" in 1939, which many believed marked the beginning of her decline. The third phase encompassed the last decade of her life, between 1949 and 1959, in which Billie Holiday was reduced to portraying Billie Holiday on the stage—in which, in other words, she came to caricature herself. Many music critics take issue with this overview and instead view Holiday's career as divided into periods of intense creativity and innovation. To compare Holiday as a young woman singing in speakeasies with Holiday at the end of her career, when her voice reflected not only the passage of time but also the ravages of drugs and alcohol, is unfair. Each period of Holiday's career was marked by highs and lows, all of which she poured into her music.

An old friend of Holiday's once remarked: "You know the kind of people that say, 'I'm gonna get cussed out anyways, so what's the difference? What the hell?' Well, Eleanora [Billie] just went out and done what she felt like doing 'cause she was just don't care-ish."[3] Billie Holiday was "just not care-ish" about many things in her life. A child of poverty, hard luck, and racism, Holiday could have turned into a hardened, bitter woman and a singer who could hide her emotions safely behind banal lyrics. She did not, and that she chose instead to create an art drawn from deep within her tormented soul is testimony as much to Holiday's talent as to her courage.

Frank O'Hara ends his elegiac poem "The Day Lady Died" with the lines "she whispered a song along the keyboard ... and everyone and I stopped breathing."[4] Such was the power, emotion, and intimacy of Holiday's music. Her troubled private life and early death have undoubtedly contributed to the aura of myth and legend that still surrounds her. Her finest performances, on the stage or in the studio, however, are among the most accomplished in the history of jazz. Her uncompromising artistry places her in the company of the best jazz and popular vocalists of the twentieth century. Billie Holiday is an American original.

NOTES

1. Quoted in Joachim-Ernst Berendt, *Jazz: A Photo History*, trans. William Odom (New York: Schirmer Books, 1979), p. 315.

2. Robert O'Meally, *Lady Day: The Many Faces of Billie Holiday* (Cambridge, MA: DeCapo Press, 1991), p. 97.

3. Buzzy Jackson, *A Bad Woman Feeling Good* (New York: W. W. Norton, 2005), p. 89.

4. Frank O'Hara, "The Day Lady Died," http://www.cs.rice.edu/~ssiyer/minstrels/poem/722.html.

TIMELINE: EVENTS IN THE LIFE OF BILLIE HOLIDAY

1915   Born Eleanora Fagan on April 7 in Philadelphia

1927   Moves with her mother Sara (Sadie) to Harlem, New York City

1929   Holiday and mother are arrested for prostitution in New York
Starts singing career at the tables of Harlem clubs

1932   Opens at Covan's nightclub on W. 132 St.

1933   Is discovered by producer John Hammond
First studio session: records first single "Your Mother's Son-in-Law"/"Riffin' the Scotch"
Signs with talent agent Joe Glaser
Records with Teddy Wilson's band under the Columbia label

1934   Performs with pianist Bobby Henderson in her first appearance at the Apollo Theatre, November 23

1935   Stars in the film *Symphony in Black* with Duke Ellington

1936   Records "Billie's Blues," her first recording as a featured solo artist

1937   Meets tenor saxophonist and lifelong friend Lester Young
Holiday's father, Clarence Holiday, dies in Texas
Tours with the Count Basie Orchestra

1938   Tours with Artie Shaw's band

1939   Opens at Café Society and records "Strange Fruit"

1941   Elopes with James Monroe
Monroe arrested on drug charges in California; Holiday goes to Hollywood to help

1942   Meets Joe Guy; begins experimenting with heroin

1944 Signs with Decca and records "Lover Man," using a string arrangement; the song is the only one she ever recorded to make the *Billboard* charts

1945 Sadie Fagan, her mother, dies

1946 First solo appearance in concert

Goes to Hollywood to star in the film *New Orleans* with Louis Armstrong

1947 Enters hospital for drug treatment

Re-signs with Decca

Arrested for drug possession and sentenced to a year in federal reformatory in Alderson, West Virginia

1948 Released from prison

Performs at a comeback concert at Carnegie Hall

Appears at the Strand Theater in "Holiday on Broadway"

1949 Arrested a second time for drug possession; is tried and acquitted

1950 Obtains divorce from Jimmy Monroe

Meets and enters into a common-law marriage with Louis McKay

1952 Begins recording for Norman Granz

1953 "Billie Holiday's Comeback Story" airs on national television

1954 Makes first concert tour of Europe

Performs at the first Newport Jazz Festival

1956 *Lady Sings the Blues* is published

Arrested for drug possession

1958 Enters studio for the last time to record *Lady in Satin*

1959 Collapses with cirrhosis; is arrested in hospital for possession of narcotics

Dies July 17, at age 47, in New York City

Chapter 1

ELEANORA

On the corner of Pennsylvania Avenue between Lanvale and Lafayette streets in Baltimore is a statue of Billie Holiday. She appears frozen in time, as if the artist had only seconds to capture the essence of his subject before she faded away. Even cast in bronze, fixed and immoveable, she remains elusive and enigmatic. Baltimore claims her now, but once, almost a century ago, Billie Holiday was among the nameless and faceless black people who lived and died without a trace. Being black and poor in Baltimore, as elsewhere throughout the United States, during the first decade of the twentieth century promised just this sort of anonymity, punctuated by hardships of various kinds. Although Maryland had remained in the Union during the Civil War (1861–1865), many white residents of the state maintained the prevailing Southern view of blacks: they were lazy, immoral, and stupid, justly consigned to lives as the hewers of wood and the drawers of water. In other words, they were suited only for performing menial tasks, and not always very reliably.

Even in freedom, blacks were condemned to lives of misery and despair. A journalist captured this sense in his description of one of the many black ghetto neighborhoods in Baltimore, very much like the one into which Billie Holiday was born. There were, he wrote "open drains ... ashes and garbage ... cellars filled with filthy black water ... villainous-looking negroes who loiter and sleep around street corners and never work ... foul streets, foul people in foul tenements filled with foul air."[1] Yet, many blacks in Baltimore did not give up hope. The promise of employment in the booming canning and shipping industries or in service to wealthy and middle-class families led many to believe they could make a better life, if not for themselves, then for their children. Among the hopeful was a luckless young woman named Sara Harris, the mother of Billie Holiday.

A ROUGH BEGINNING

Sara Harris's life began in humble circumstances. Born on August 18, 1896, to Charles Fagan and a woman now known only by her surname, Harris, Sara herself knew little about her origins or background. Soon after her birth, her father had left Baltimore, but he later returned and married a laundress from Virginia named Martha "Mattie" Dixon. Throughout most of his life, Charles Fagan worked as a waiter in several Baltimore hotels. At some point, he found a job as an elevator operator in the B&O (Baltimore and Ohio Railroad) Building in the heart of Baltimore's downtown business district. Through their labors, Charles and Mattie not only attained a certain measure of financial security, but they also in time were able to move from the East Side slums to a home in a respectable black neighborhood in West Baltimore.

Mattie Fagan ruled her household. Not only did she persuade her husband to convert to Catholicism, but she also made certain that he worked hard and regularly brought home a paycheck. Mattie wanted her family to be prosperous and respectable. She had no time for her in-laws, whom she regarded as ne'er-do-wells, and she rarely accompanied her husband to visit the old neighborhood or to see his siblings. She did not extend the hospitality of her home to the Fagans. Of course, she had nothing whatsoever to do with Charles's illegitimate daughter, Sara Harris.

GOD BLESS THE CHILD

In an attempt to draw closer to her father, Sara, or Sadie as she became known, converted to Catholicism. It did her little good; for the rest of her life she remained outside the family. Even the Fagans did not accept her.

Eventually, Sara Harris found work as a live-in maid for a wealthy white family. Sometime during the summer of 1914, when she was 18, Sara went to a carnival or a dance where she met and was seduced by Clarence Holiday, a 16-year-old grocery delivery boy and aspiring musician who lived at home with his parents. Shortly thereafter, Sadie learned that she was pregnant. She left Baltimore for Philadelphia, paying for her trip by taking what was known as a transportation job, a form of employment in which a white person paid for the travel of an African American in exchange for services rendered on the trip. Upon her arrival in Philadelphia, Sadie moved into a room at 1131 South Broad Street and soon found work as a domestic.

However, her pregnancy and her status as a single woman soon led her employers to fire her. With no money and no one to turn to, Sadie went to Philadelphia General Hospital, where in exchange for scrubbing floors and waiting on patients, she received medical care during the remaining months of her pregnancy.

In Philadelphia General Hospital at 2:30 on the morning of April 7, 1915, Sara Harris gave birth to a daughter, whom she named Eleanora. The father of record listed on Eleanora's birth certificate was Frank DeViese, a 20-year-old waiter who had befriended Sadie and who was at the hospital when Sadie gave birth.

Not long after, Sadie turned to her half-sister Eva in Baltimore, asking for her help in taking care of Eleanora. Eva agreed and sent her husband, Robert Miller, to Philadelphia to pick up the infant and return to Baltimore. His trip marked the beginning of an unhappy pattern in Eleanora's life, as she was often shunted between relatives and friends while Sadie was off working. She did not stay with the Millers long; Eva and Robert were trying to start their own family. Eleanora was then placed with Miller's mother, Martha, who took care of the child for the first 18 months of her life.

"AMERICA'S CLASSICAL MUSIC"

"If the truth were known about the origin of 'jazz,'" wrote musician Clay Smith in 1924, "it would never be mentioned in polite society."[2] The word was African American slang for copulation, used both as a noun and a verb. The term later came to mean a sense of excitement, energy, and invigoration. In its various forms—jass, jasz, and jaz are among the early spellings—jazz may have derived from a West African dialect, though no connection has ever been proven.

The association of *jazz* with a particular kind of music is hardly surprising, considering that music played in the jazz style originated in the steamy atmosphere of New Orleans bars and bordellos. One of the first recorded identifications of jazz as a musical form came in 1917 from reporter Lafcadio Hearn, who worked for a Cincinnati newspaper. Filing dispatches from New Orleans, Hearn reported that the "word 'jaz,' meaning to speed things up, to make excitement, [was] common among the blacks of the South and had been adopted by the Creoles as a term to be applied to music of a rudimentary syncopated type."[3]

It was against the backdrop of deepening racial animosity and violence that jazz emerged. The promise of racial emancipation and equality had disappeared with the end of Reconstruction in 1877, and, as a result, blacks, especially in the South, witnessed the erosion of their rights. The Supreme Court decision in the case of *Plessy v. Ferguson* (1896) legalized racial discrimination by formally embracing the doctrine of "separate-but-equal." Violence against blacks increased dramatically; even those spared the worst abuses suffered the misery of poverty, fear, and hopelessness. According to writer Richard Knight, for these reasons jazz is a "heroic" music. An original American art form, jazz, Knight declared, told the story of how:

> The USA's most marginalised and oppressed people, black slaves and their descendants, defied the indignity of their situation to make, through music, a contribution to world culture which would eclipse every other art form in the USA. So great was this sound, jazz and blues, it has informed the subsequent development of all popular music.[4]

In addition, he continued, jazz revealed the dignity and feeling of a people and a race:

> Jazz is something Negroes invented, and it said the most profound things.... It is the nobility of the race put into sound.... Jazz has all the elements, from the spare and penetrating to the complex and enveloping. It is the hardest music to play that I know of, and it is the highest rendition of individual emotion in the history of Western music.[5]

Jazz is a hybrid; it has no single origin. It combines African rhythms with Western harmonies. However, it was African music, with its complex polyrhythmic structure, that provided the heart and soul of jazz. Thus, even as it incorporated many elements of Western music, jazz represented a break from Western musical styles and traditions. The music of an oppressed and downtrodden people, jazz allowed for a great deal of freedom to express ideas, moods, and emotions—freedoms otherwise denied to black people. To some extent, all music is improvised; even classical musicians rarely, if ever, play the same piece in exactly the same way. Yet, it is hard to imagine any music that gives the players as much freedom to improvise as jazz does. For example, the great tenor saxophonist Lester Young, who collaborated with Billie Holiday on some of her most memorable work, developed his own improvised system of harmony that he applied no matter what the key or the chords of the song.[6] Jazz was more than a mixing of styles and rhythms. It was the result of distinctive ethnic, cultural, and social conditions found only in the United States, and specifically, in New Orleans.

THE SPIRITUAL CENTER

Jazz arose in the United States not by chance, but because of a unique set of social, economic, intellectual, and spiritual conditions that existed nowhere else. At the turn of the twentieth century, blacks constituted approximately 10 percent of the American population. Largely excluded from the mainstream of national life, these people had developed a culture of their own, which included distinctive musical forms that in time became popular with other groups. One theory to explain why New Orleans was the birthplace of jazz is that the men and women, black, white, and mixed, who lived there had long heard ragtime being played and were prepared to take the next step in the evolution of music.[7]

With the establishment of Storyville, the legendary red-light, or prostitution, district of New Orleans, in 1897, jazz took root and flourished. Bounded by Basin and Robertson streets, and extending from Perdido to Gravier streets, Storyville was home to more than 2,000 registered prostitutes who plied their trade in dozens of brothels. In such houses of ill repute, and in the dance halls and dives they supported, jazz was born.

Yet, New Orleans, with its diverse population that includes French, Spanish, and English peoples as well as Africans, is more a Caribbean than a North American city. Jazz might have remained a local phenomenon, like so many other New Orleans specialties from jambalaya to etoufée, from boudin to voodoo, had not attitudes throughout the United States become more accommodating to jazz. The emergence of a complex set of ideas and values called *modernism* made jazz acceptable to a wider audience. Modernism helped to break down an older way of thinking and living known as Victorianism, which emphasized order, decency, honor, self-control, hard work, and respectability. By the late nineteenth and early twentieth centuries, many Americans, especially members of the younger generation, found Victorian reserve unbearably staid and oppressive. They sought the freedom to express themselves intellectually, emotionally, artistically, and sexually. Because it seemed to embody this new spirit of freedom, jazz appealed to those who embraced modernism.

As the South became less attractive to blacks, many decided to move North. They brought jazz with them. In the northeastern United States, a "sizzling" new style of playing developed. Although the center of the new music was New York City, it appeared elsewhere, including Baltimore. This music was characterized by rollicking rhythms, but lacked the distinctly bluesy influence that dominated southern jazz. In Baltimore's black community, jazz was soon heard everywhere. Jazz singer Ruby Glover recalled the energy of "the Avenue," the main thoroughfare of Old West, one of the city's oldest black neighborhoods:

> When you went in there they were always talking about who was up the street, or who was playing, or don't forget there's a dance at the corner. There was always a conversation in every little pocket, where you saw people talking. They were telling each other, remember to come out because so and so is going to be there. Don't forget to go up the street because the Casino's got so and so.[8]

Baltimore produced a number of prominent young jazz musicians, including pianist Eubie Blake, drummer Chick Webb, bandleader Elmer Snowden, and a young guitarist named Clarence Holiday.

"I'M A DADDY NOW"

The son of Nelson Holliday, a hospital laborer, and Mary Johnston, a laundress, Clarence Holliday was born on July 23, 1898. It is unclear how or when Clarence became interested in music, but by 1917, though still living with his parents, he began to find jobs playing banjo and guitar. Clarence delivered groceries to pay for music lessons.

In 1917 at the height of hostilities in Europe, Clarence, then working as an elevator operator, decided to enlist in the U.S. Army under the name Clarence Holiday, dropping the second "l" in his surname. In addition, he gave military officials his birth year as 1895 instead of 1898, which would have made him too young to sign up. On November 27, 1917, two days after being assigned the rank of private, Holiday deserted his regiment in Washington, D.C. A year later in August, Holiday was inducted into the army again and sent to the 54th Company, 153rd Depot Brigade. By October 1918, Holiday was settled into his new job as bugler for Company I, 811 Pion Infantry and headed to France. Not long after their arrival, the war ended. Holiday would leave France in June 1919 and return home to Baltimore.

Later in life, Holiday claimed he had been the victim of a poison gas attack. In fact, his daughter would later claim that her father died as a result of lingering complications from that experience. However, there is no record of Holiday having suffered from such an attack; his tale became one more legend interwoven within Billie Holiday's own tangled life.

Soon, Clarence found steady work as a banjo and guitar player, playing with different bands. He toured with Billy Fowler, Fletcher Henderson, Don Redmon, and McKinney's Cotton Pickers. His playing abilities were such that his stature as a musician rose.

In 1920, Sadie returned to Baltimore and took up residence at Eva and Robert's house near the city's downtown, where she was reunited with her daughter. Under the name of Sadie Fagan, she found work in a shirt factory. Eva, who now had two children of her own, tended to Eleanora. Although Sadie's father, Charles, was unhappy at Sadie's taking on the Fagan name, his concern for the welfare of his daughter and granddaughter led him to look in on them on rare occasions. Charles was not the only visitor; Clarence Holiday, hearing that Sadie had returned to Baltimore, occasionally visited the Miller home, though he discouraged Sadie's attempts to draw him back into a relationship or, worse, matrimony.

Her father's refusal to marry Sadie preyed on Billie Holiday's psyche. In her autobiography, *Lady Sings the Blues,* Billie recalled that her parents finally married when she was three. "Mom and Pop were just a couple of kids when they got married," she wrote. "He was eighteen, she was sixteen, and I was three." But the fact remains that her parents never married. Even when her mother died, Holiday asked that she be acknowledged as Clarence's widow. The harsh reality remained that Clarence kept both Sadie and Eleanora in the background, refusing to acknowledge to his family that he even had a daughter, though he told his friend Elmer Snowden, "You know, I'm a daddy now." Snowden later met Eleanora when she was three, and described her as "an ugly little thing, a homely looking baby."[9]

Clarence Holiday's rising fame as a musician gave him the excuse he needed to be away from Sadie and Eleanora. For his young daughter, he remained always a shadowy presence. Sadie did her best to keep track of her wayward lover. She took transportation jobs, not only because they paid better than domestic service, but also because they enabled her to keep an eye on Clarence. Clarence did his best to hide from Sadie, sometimes going so far as to change the spelling of his name. In 1922, he married Helen Boudin and moved to Philadelphia and out of his daughter's life.

SEARCHING FOR RESPECTABILITY

After learning of Clarence's marriage, Sadie returned to domestic service and did her best to support Eleanora. She refused to allow poverty to dampen their spirits or destroy their lives. But no matter how hard Sadie worked, there was never enough money.

In October 1920, life seemed to take a turn for the better when Sadie met and married a 25-year-old longshoreman named Philip Gough. To help out the newlyweds, Charles Fagan offered them a house, located on North Fremont Street in West Baltimore. For almost three years, Sadie and Eleanora had some security. Then Gough abandoned his family. As Sadie fell further behind on the house payments, Charles Fagan took over the mortgage. Sadie and Eleanora, however, had to move out. For Eleanora, the Fagans' rejection of both her and her mother was a wound that never healed. Years later, when, as a famous singer, Billie Holiday returned to Baltimore, she made no effort to see her Fagan relatives.

THE POINT

Despite the collapse of her marriage, Sadie had to think about her daughter's welfare. She was concerned about Eleanora's education, for by the time Eleanora was in the fourth grade, she began skipping school as often as possible. Caught by a local truant officer, Eleanora was ordered to appear in juvenile court. The judge deemed that the nine-year-old lacked proper parental care and supervision, and in January 1925 sent her to the House of Good Shepherd for Colored Girls, a Catholic school for wayward girls and young women. As the youngest of the girls at Good Shepherd, Eleanora was easy sexual prey for the older girls; several writers have suggested that Eleanora was introduced to lesbianism at Good Shepherd, which may in part explain her bisexuality.

In October 1925, after 10 months at Good Shepherd, Eleanora returned to her mother's custody. The two moved again, this time to an area near the docks known as Fells Point, which was then a red-light district filled with brothels and bars. Sadie arranged to sublet a small apartment, which allowed her kitchen privileges. Residents of the neighborhood remember her as a small, neat woman, a good cook, and a churchgoer who attended Mass at the nearby Catholic Church. Sadie still worked as a domestic whenever she could. However, because money was scarce, she relied more fully on better-paying transportation jobs, which kept her away for home for several days at a time. During Sadie's frequent absences, neighbors looked in on Eleanora.

At some point, Sadie began a relationship with a local tough named Wee Wee Hill. Hill moved mother and daughter to a second-floor apartment in a building that his mother owned. Sadie tried various ways to increase her income. Not only did she continue to work as a domestic, but for a short time, she may also have operated a small restaurant out of her apartment. The fare was pig's feet, red beans, and rice, with bootleg whiskey served in the living room. The restaurant was only open in the evenings, which allowed Sadie to work during the day. Sadie's hard work made her one of the few neighborhood residents who could afford both gas and electricity.

Yet, Sadie's bad luck with men continued. Hill refused to marry her and continued to see other women. Sadie eventually went to New York to look for better-paying work. Eleanora stayed behind in the care of Hill's mother, Lucy.

LEARNING LIFE'S LESSONS

For the most part, 10-year-old Eleanora was left to fend for herself. Miss Lu was infirm and could do little to control her. Mature for her age, and already showing signs of becoming a beautiful woman, Eleanora looked elsewhere for a role model. She found one in Ethel Moore, a successful businesswoman who owned one of the more profitable brothels in the Point. To earn extra cash, Eleanora worked for Ethel, doing odd jobs and domestic chores. Without much supervision of any kind, Eleanora did what she wanted, when she wanted. Her mother's misfortunes with men made a deep impression on Eleanora. She did not want to be pushed around, subject to the whims of others. She began to develop a tougher, harder view of life, the world, and men. Resolving never to endure rejection from a man, Eleanora had a series of brief relationships and broke up with her boyfriends before they had the chance to break up with her.

THE EVOLUTION OF A SINGER

Busy as she was, Eleanora found time to pursue the one interest that she seemed to love: singing. Taking advantage of every opportunity to sing, Eleanora began to perform in local amateur shows at movie houses as well as in a number of the storefront churches located throughout black neighborhoods. She also spent time at Ethel Moore's brothel, which housed a Victrola. Sitting in the upstairs bar, she first heard the music of such artists as Bessie Smith and Louis Armstrong.

These recordings were "race records," which recording companies had developed in the 1920s to expand sales to blacks. The phenomenal success of Mamie Smith's 1920 hit "Crazy Blues," which sold more than 500,000 copies, boosted the careers of other black singers and musicians, whose talents the record companies had previously ignored. Of all the singers she listened to, Bessie Smith was Eleanora's favorite. Although Holiday always denied that she was a blues singer, her style, strongly influenced by Bessie Smith, was grounded in the blues tradition. Horn players, such as trumpeter Louis Armstrong, also influenced Holiday's singing. Armstrong was among the first to develop improvisation and scat singing. According to jazz critic and historian Stanley Crouch, "Armstrong, like Bessie Smith, was a master of inflection, capable of coming down on a note in almost endless ways, to the extent that one tone could jab, bite, simmer, dissolve, swell, yelp, sizzle, or grind."[10] Holiday always credited the development of her singing style to both Smith and Armstrong, stating in one interview that "I got my manner from Bessie Smith and Louis Armstrong, honey. I wanted [Bessie's] feeling and Louis' style."[11]

Eleanora picked up singing jobs wherever she could, sometimes performing at several clubs in one evening. She took care of herself, rarely drinking and only occasionally smoking marijuana. Her light complexion, almost straight black hair worn in a bun or a pageboy, statuesque figure, and comely face made her a favorite with the men who frequented in the Point. Women, however, were jealous of her, and Eleanora learned early on how to defend herself against their attacks.

Concerned with Eleanora's behavior and for her welfare, Miss Lu wrote to Sadie, asking her to send for her daughter. According to Wee Wee Hill, Eleanora was happy to go to New York. And so it was that in early 1929, wearing a white voile dress with a red shiny belt, Eleanora Harris left Baltimore for New York City. It was almost four years before she would return to Baltimore, not as Eleanora Harris, but as Billie Holiday.

NOTES

1. Donald Clarke, *Wishing on the Moon: The Life and Times of Billie Holiday* (New York: Viking, 1994), p. 6.

2. Hugh Rawson, "Jazz," *American Heritage* (October 2004): p. 18.

3. Ibid.

4. Richard Knight, "All That Jazz," *Geographical* (October 2001): p. 14.

5. Wynton Marsalis, quoted in Ken Burns and Geoffrey C. Ward, *Jazz—A History of America's Music* (New York: Knopf, 2000), p. 25.

6. Lewis Porter, *Lester Young* (Boston: Twayne, 1985), pp. 66–67. Despite the prevailing emphasis on improvisation, James Lincoln Collier argues persuasively that most "improvised" jazz solos are transcribed and memorized, and that not until 1923 did the improvised solo become the central component of jazz. Before 1923, ensemble playing predominated. See *Jazz: The American Theme Song* (New York: Oxford University Press, 1993), pp. 25–27.

7. See James Lincoln Collier, *The Making of Jazz: A Comprehensive History* (New York: Delta, 1979), pp. 57–71.

8. Joel D. Miller, "The Rise and Fall of Jazz in Baltimore," http://www.american.edu/bgriff/h481 web/History%20Day%20Power%20Points/miller.ppt.

9. Clarke, *Wishing on the Moon*, p. 11.

10. Stanley Crouch, "Louis Armstrong," *Time*, June 8, 1998, p. 170.

11. Clarke, *Wishing on the Moon*, p. 36.

Chapter 2

BILLIE

Uncertainties, inaccuracies, and discrepancies abound in the story of Billie Holiday. No one, for example, knows exactly when she arrived in New York City. Some accounts give the date as 1927; others place her arrival sometime in 1929. Whatever the date, her trip was not without mishap. She missed her original stop, where Sadie was waiting, and instead got off the train in Harlem, where she became lost. When local authorities picked her up, Eleanora refused to cooperate. She would not even tell them her name.

Finally reunited with her mother, Eleanora moved to Harlem where Sadie had rented rooms at 151 West 140th Street, between Lenox and Seventh avenues. The building was home to Florence Williams, a noted Harlem madam. To earn money, Sadie had begun to work for Williams, and in a short time, Eleanora also became one of Williams's girls. At 14, she earned five dollars for every trick she turned.

THE NEGRO CAPITAL OF THE WORLD

Harlem in the 1920s was the most famous black neighborhood in the United States. Bounded by 110th Street and running north to 155th Street, bordered on the west by Morningside Drive and St. Nicholas Avenue and on the east by the East River, Harlem had once been a white neighborhood, populated, as the name suggests, mainly by Dutch immigrants. With the introduction of commuter rail service during the 1870s, Harlem evolved from an isolated, impoverished village in the northern reaches of Manhattan into a wealthy residential suburb.

When the Lenox Avenue subway line opened in the early years of the twentieth century, a flurry of real estate speculation contributed to a substantial increase in construction. At that time, the population of Harlem was largely English and German, with increasing numbers of Jewish immigrants. By 1904, however, the economic prosperity had come to an end, largely as the result of high rents and excessive construction. In that same year, Phillip A. Payton, Jr., a black realtor, founded the Afro-American Realty Company with the intention of leasing vacant white-owned buildings and then renting them to blacks. Although Payton's company survived only four years, it played a pivotal role in opening Harlem up to black residents.

The massive exodus of blacks from the South during the early years of the century also dramatically altered the ethnic composition of Harlem, until, by 1930, it had become a predominately black enclave. In 1890 there had been approximately 25,000 blacks living in Manhattan. By 1910 that number had more than tripled to 90,000. In the following decade, the black population increased to approximately 150,000 and, by 1930, had more than doubled to 325,000. In Harlem itself, the black population rose from approximately 50,000 in 1914 to about 80,000 in 1920 to almost 200,000 by 1930. From a social perspective, Harlem was a city within a city. By the 1920s, moreover, Harlem had come to occupy an important place in American intellectual and political history, thanks in part to the Harlem Renaissance, a cultural ferment that gained black art, music, and literature a wider audience and greater acceptance.

By the 1910s, Harlem had already become the entertainment capital of black America. Ballrooms, speakeasies (places where customers could buy illegal liquor), nightclubs, whorehouses, and drug dens proliferated. With the coming of Prohibition in 1919, whites converged on Harlem. "Slumming" in search of illicit excitement and illegal pleasure became a favorite pastime for uptown whites. Eleanora was swept up in the energy of her new home. "Every night limousines would wheel uptown," she recalled. "The minks and ermines would climb over one another to be the first one through the coalbins or over the garbage pails into the newest spot that was 'the place.'"[1]

A NEW WORLD

Like black writers and artists, black musicians also gravitated to Harlem. Willie "the Lion" Smith, Fats Waller, and James P. Johnson created an early version of jazz piano known as the Harlem Stride around the time of World War I. After 1920, bandleaders such as Fletcher Henderson, Duke Ellington, and Chick Webb laid the foundation for swing and big-band jazz. Whites flocked to Harlem to hear jazz. When Duke Ellington and his orchestra played at the Cotton Club—the most famous nightspot in Harlem located at 644 Lenox Avenue—wealthy white New Yorkers filled the place, enthralled by the music and at the spectacle of the feathered black and tan dancers.

Just down the street from the Cotton Club, at 596 Lennox Avenue, was the Savoy Ballroom. Nicknamed "the Home of the Happy Feet," the Savoy became the hottest dance hall in town, drawing throngs of blacks and whites alike.[2] Many dance crazes of the 1920s and 1930s originated there. The ballroom itself was majestic. Patrons entered by a marble-pillared staircase lit by cut-glass chandeliers that led into the massive orange and blue dance hall. The management of the Savoy was known for having invented the "Battle of the Bands," which pitted one band against another. Each band played on a revolving stage located at opposite ends of the hall; as one band ended a song, the other band began to play, guaranteeing that the music was nonstop. For an aspiring singer such as Eleanora Harris, Harlem was the place to be. There was no place on earth quite like it.

WORKING GIRL

On May 2, 1929, Eleanora was arrested on charges of prostitution. In *Wishing on the Moon*, Donald Clarke, one of her biographers, explained that the incident occurred when she refused to serve a wealthy black customer who retaliated by having her arrested.[3] Other sources give a different account of the episode. They state that Eleanora, her mother, Florence Williams, and 22 other prostitutes were arrested during a police raid on the Williams establishment. In the police report, Eleanora gave her name as Eleanora Fagan, declaring that she was 21 years old.

All the women were jailed overnight; the following morning, all were scheduled to appear in the Women's Night Court of the Magistrate's Court for the Ninth District of Manhattan. All were charged with vagrancy; however, the sentences varied. Some of the women were released; two others, including Florence Williams, were sent to the workhouse. Facing the wrath of a stern woman judge, Eleanora was sentenced to 100 days at Welfare Island, now Roosevelt Island, located in the East River. The island facilities consisted of a workhouse and a hospital; most of its residents were prostitutes and drug addicts. By October, Eleanora was back with Sadie, who had moved to a new apartment at 7 Glenada Avenue in Brooklyn.

It was at this time that Eleanora struck up a friendship with a Kenneth Holton, a struggling saxophone player who lived nearby. Sadie had returned to working as a domestic; Eleanora, though, decided she would "never scrub floors or keep house for white folks."[4] She was going to become a singer and spent her days singing along with Holton, beginning a lifelong love affair with the saxophone and those who played it. At night, she began making the rounds of the local hotspots looking for work.

Early in 1930, Holton got Eleanora her first professional singing job at the Grey Dawn, a small cabaret in Queens. Singing Fats Waller's "My Fate Is in Your Hands" and "How Am I to Know" with the Hat Hunter band, Eleanora so impressed the audience that they threw money on the floor. Soon Holton and Eleanora were working in clubs in Harlem and Brooklyn as well as holding down a regular appearance at the local Elks Club. Their informal arrangement, however, ended in spring of 1930 when Sadie decided to move back to Harlem and take a new job.

MEET BILLIE HOLIDAY

Mae Barnes, a singer and dancer who worked in black vaudeville, remembered the first time she heard Billie Holiday sing. Both women were performing at the Nest Club. Billie, Barnes said:

> wasn't doing her own style. She was doing everything that Louis Armstrong was doing. She knew his records backwards.... She wasn't imitatin' his style, she was using all his numbers. That was her beginnin' of changing Louis's style to her own.... She had this heavy voice, this gravelly tone.[5]

Around the time she appeared at the Nest Club, Eleanora decided to change her name. The most popular version of the story is that Eleanora called herself "Billie" after one of her favorite actors, Billie Dove, "the American Beauty," a popular white star of silent films.[6] Billie Dove, who began life as Lillian Bohny, was born in New York in 1900. At 17, she became a member of the famous Ziegfeld Follies, and then went to Hollywood where she enjoyed success as a movie star. She was at the peak of her popularity in 1923, playing against such Hollywood greats as Douglas Fairbanks. Dove was often cast as the maiden in distress who was always rescued at the last moment by the handsome hero. She retired from making films in 1935 and pursued other interests, among them, flying planes, painting, and writing.

According to Mae Barnes, however, Eleanora did not change her name because of Billie Dove, but rather because of a friend named Billie. She had no reason to take Fagan as her surname given her relatives' dislike of her and her mother. Though reluctant to take advantage of her father's growing fame as a jazz musician, Billie took "Holiday" as her last name. For a short time, however, she spelled it "Halliday."

THE "UP" GIRL

Billie and other young, female singers on the after-hours club circuit had a regular routine. They began work at two in the morning and finished between seven and eight. Afterward, they headed to one or another of the small bars where they could drink and visit until around noon. Then, they usually went to someone's apartment to continue drinking and often to take drugs. By four or five in the afternoon, the girls finally went to bed. There was no let-up to this grueling schedule, for the singers worked seven days a week, earning about $100 each.

Called "ups" because each would get up on stage to sing only a few songs at a time before yielding to another singer, the girls went from table to table collecting tips from the customers. Patrons laid the money on the table, and the girls had to clamp their thighs around it to pick it up. Billie refused, finding the practice insulting and degrading. Instead, she received her tips by hand or did not take them at all. She also refused requests to sing dirty songs or to accept dates. By this time, Billie was determined to make money standing on her feet, not lying on her back. She would not take money for prostituting herself. Club owners, customers, and many of the other singers thought that Billie was arrogant, allegedly prompting some of the girls mockingly to call her "Lady Day," one explanation of how Billie acquired her famous moniker.

Billie did not much care what others thought of her. She was no longer the unwanted child, the truant, or the wayward young girl. Recognizing her gift, Billie was working hard to make a name for herself as a singer. Yet, trouble still found her. In 1930, she was again arrested, this time on charges of public drunkenness and disorderly conduct. As she became more famous, her brushes with the law became more frequent.

MAKING HER WAY

At the same time that Billie embarked on a singing career, the economy collapsed, triggering the worst depression in American history.

The economic downturn was hard on almost everyone, including those who owned nightclubs, cabarets, and record companies. Many went out of business. For thousands of blacks, the Great Depression was nothing really new: money had always been scarce and jobs hard to come by. They had long depended on luck, cunning, and perseverance to make their way in the world.

By the summer of 1930, Billie and Sadie were living in a tiny room in Harlem on West 27th Street, between Lenox and Fifth avenues. Because singing jobs were even harder to come by than usual, Billie went to work as a waitress at Mexico's, a Harlem restaurant and nightclub where Sadie worked as a cook. Alto saxophonist Benny Carter remembered the place as being popular with many local musicians. The owner allowed Billie to supplement her income by singing at the tables for extra tips. This experience proved more valuable than the little money she earned. Not only did she learn how to establish immediate intimacy with an audience, but she also learned how to vary her style, never twice singing the same song in the same way.

In her spare time, Billie associated with the musicians who came into Mexico's. Many remembered her as beautiful and shy, but easy to talk to:

> She spoke in practically a whisper ....She was an uncompromising, devastatingly honest kind of girl ... very attractive, very cool, very gentle ... an extremely quiet person who liked to laugh ... She had a gingham gown on her and she was vivacious and young and nice.... She was like sunshine![7]

Finally, Billie got the break for which she had been waiting. One night at Mexico's, Marge Johnson, an established blues singer, heard Billie singing. She told Charlie Johnson, who headed the house band at the popular nightspot Ed Small's Paradise to schedule an audition for Billie. Contrary to its name, Small's club was the big time. The place seated almost 1,500 persons, and whites from uptown were frequent patrons. Billie failed the audition. "I got there," she recounted:

> and I'm all ready to sing and this cat asks me, 'What key you singin' in?' I said, 'I don't know man, you just play.' They shooed me out of there so fast it wasn't even funny ... From then on I'd start remembering and I would pitch my keys.[8]

Disappointed as she must have been, Billie pushed on, landing small singing jobs here and there. Benny Carter recalled seeing Billie sing at the

Bright Spot, a club on Seventh Avenue and West 139th Street. Carter, renowned for his elegant playing, composing, and arranging, admired Billie's voice, style, and presence. He recalled that she was "not the typical blues singer" nor was she "just another singer." Like so many others, Carter did not know quite what to make of the young woman who had already begun to shape her own sound. She fit no category. Carter admitted that he did not know if he had ever "heard anything like that [before] … or indeed since."[9]

ENTERING THE WORLD

As Billie's contacts with musicians increased, she began to drink more and to take more drugs. She began to smoke marijuana, known as "weed," "grass," "tea," or "reefer," more regularly. At that time, marijuana was relatively cheap; one could purchase two "joints" for twenty-five cents (approximately two dollars in today's currency).

Despite her indulgence in drugs and alcohol, Billie never turned down a chance to sing. Singing became her classroom; each song offered another lesson about music. She paid close attention to each instrument, especially when musicians would begin improvising, using tone and characteristic riffs to imprint a song with their signature style. By imitating, and drawing elements from, other people's styles, Billie began to create her own unique approach to singing. Within two years, her reputation as a singer had spread throughout Harlem, and she got regular bookings at clubs, cabarets, and bars.

DADDY

The world of jazz musicians is small and insular. It was thus only a matter of time before Billie met her father. Clarence Holiday worked with noted bandleader Fletcher Henderson. In 1932, Holiday also began playing at Bert Hall's Rhythm Club, a Harlem gathering place for musicians to meet and look for work. At some point, Billie met her father, though accounts of their meeting differ. In her autobiography, Billie wrote that her first meeting with her father came not long after she and Sadie had moved back to Harlem. Clarence was working with Henderson's band at the Roseland Ballroom. With money tight, Billie more than once went to the Roseland to ask her father for help:

> I used to go right down there and haunt him. Pop was in his early
> thirties then, but he didn't want anyone to guess it—especially

the young chicks who used to hang around the entrance waiting
for the musicians.... I'd try to catch his eye and call out to him,
'Hey Daddy.' I soon found out just waving at him would make
him feel forty-five, and he didn't like that.[10]

Pleading with his daughter not to call him "Daddy," Clarence gave
Billie money perhaps just to be rid of her. By this time, though, those
who knew them both understood that Clarence was Billie's father. Clara
Winston, one of the leading madams of Harlem during the Depression,
recalled in an interview that Billie looked just like her father, "only she
was taller and he was a little shorter. But they had the same freaky-looking
eyes, sort of slanty eyes."[11]

Although some described the relationship between Billie and her father as distant and strained, others saw it as amicable. Clarence seems
to have cared deeply for his daughter. He told his boyhood friend, Elmer
Snowden, who was also living in Harlem, to take good care of his little girl
whenever Clarence left to go on the road.

JOHN HAMMOND

Toward the end of 1932, Billie had the opportunity to sing at a small
club called Covan's on West 132nd Street. She was replacing Monette
Moore, a popular jazz singer who had taken a role on the Broadway stage.
Moore was a powerful performer, known for her low, growling voice.

One of Moore's biggest fans was a young man named John Hammond.
Born in 1910 in New York City, Hammond was the great-grandson of the
wealthy tycoon William Henry Vanderbilt. As a youngster, Hammond
showed great interest in music; by the age of four, he was studying piano,
and at eight, he learned to play the violin. By the time he was in his teens,
Hammond had developed a deep interest in black music and soon became
a familiar sight in the many clubs and theaters of Harlem.

In 1928 Hammond entered Yale University, where he continued to play
the violin, and, later, the viola. Hammond soon dropped out of school
and traveled to England where he became a reporter for the popular
music magazine *Melody Maker*. During one of his many visits to Covan's,
Hammond developed a deep admiration for Monette Moore's singing.
In early 1933, Hammond stopped at Covan's expecting to hear Moore
perform. He was interested in establishing himself as a music promoter
and producer, and, perhaps, thought about taking on Moore as a client.
(In fact, one of Hammond's earliest recording ventures was a series of
records featuring Garland Wilson, Moore's pianist.)

Instead of Moore, though, Hammond heard Billie Holiday for the first time. As Holiday began singing the popular "Wouldja for a Big Red Apple?", Hammond was transfixed. He realized he was listening to a singer unlike any other he had heard. As he watched Billie move from table to table, improvising the song, Hammond later stated, "The way she sang around a melody, her uncanny harmonic sense and her sense of lyric content was almost unbelievable in a girl of seventeen."[12] Yet, despite thinking that Holiday was a special singer, Hammond decided to get a second opinion. He asked his close friends Red Norvo, an accomplished jazz musician, and his wife, singer Mildred Bailey, to come with him to hear Billie. Together the trio visited Covan's as well as a number of the smaller clubs where Billie performed. When Bailey heard Holiday, she exclaimed to Hammond: "This girl can sing!"[13] Hammond wasted no time; as soon as he could, he introduced himself to Billie. It was the beginning of a rewarding collaboration.

NOTES

1. Billie Holiday, with William Dufty, *Lady Sings the Blues* (New York: Penguin, 1992), p. 23.

2. Kennedy Center for the Arts, "Drop Me Off in Harlem," http://artsedge.kennedy-center.org/exploring/harlem/placesmain_text.html.

3. Donald Clarke, *Wishing on the Moon: The Life and Times of Billie Holiday* (New York: Viking, 1994), p. 49.

4. Stuart Nicholson, *Billie Holiday* (Boston: Northeastern University Press, 1994), p. 33.

5. Clarke, *Wishing on the Moon*, p. 47.

6. Julia Blackburn, *With Billie* (New York: Pantheon, 2005), p. 63.

7. John Chilton, *Billie's Blues* (New York: Stein and Day, 1975), p. 22.

8. Billie Holiday, *The Complete Billie Holiday on Verve, 1945–1959*, 517658-2. Disc 4, track 32.

9. Nicholson, *Billie Holiday*, p. 36.

10. Holiday, *Lady Sings the Blues*, p. 33.

11. Blackburn, *With Billie*, p. 74.

12. Nicholson, *Billie Holiday*, p. 39.

13. Ibid., p. 40.

Chapter 3

LADIES AND GENTLEMEN ...
BILLIE HOLIDAY

Years later, John Hammond wrote about Billie Holiday: "My discovery of Billie Holiday was the kind of accident I dreamed of … the sort of reward I received now and then by traveling to every place where anyone performed."[1] It was becoming clear to Hammond and to others who heard Billie sing that she offered something new and fresh. It marked the beginning of a vocal styling that experimented, challenged, and captivated audiences and musicians alike.

Unlike many singers who simply worked to entertain an audience by giving them what they wanted to hear, Billie's singing conveyed much more. Her voice was full of expression as she interpreted the music in her own way. She mimicked the sound of the instruments accompanying her, and took chances with a song's lyrics, playing with the words to create something new and unique. More than one person commented on her ability to take even the silliest of songs and inject them with new life and meaning.

For discerning listeners such as John Hammond, Billie's singing marked a more sophisticated approach to jazz. Billie did not want to entertain the audience; she sought to communicate with them. Each note she sang was an expression of Billie's own life, her own experiences, and, as time went on, her own misery and despair. For Billie Holiday, singing was sharing her heart and soul with her listeners.

WORKING HER WAY ALONG

When her engagement at Covan's ended, Billie returned to Mexico's, where Sadie was still working in the kitchen. Not long after she returned, the ownership of the restaurant changed hands. The new owner refused to pay Billie the two week's salary that was owed to her. Billie's temper got the better of her; she and Sadie were fired. With both out of work, mother and daughter struggled again to make ends meet. Unwilling to go back to waiting on tables, Billie started to work her way around the clubs, trying desperately to find a regular singing job. After a day of rejections, Billie walked into a popular establishment known as the Catagonia Club, or Pod's and Jerry's to its regulars, on West 133rd Street. Jerry Preston, one of the owners, let Billie audition. He was impressed enough with her abilities that he offered her a job for two dollars a night plus tips. Billie accepted; shortly thereafter, Sadie landed a job in the kitchen.

Located in the basement of a brownstone, Pod's and Jerry's was one of the hottest places in Harlem to hear jazz. When whites visiting from the more fashionable neighborhoods of the city arrived in their sleek limousines, the headman, George Woods, escorted them to their seats. From two to seven in the morning, Pod's and Jerry's exploded with music from jazz bands accompanied by singing and dancing. The informal master of ceremonies was the piano player Willie "the Lion" Smith. It was generally acknowledged that if people loved nightlife, they always included a stop at Pod's and Jerry's before heading home.

BOBBY

At Pod's and Jerry's, Billie soon clashed with Willie Smith's accompaniment, calling it old-fashioned. She wanted a more modern pianist, a stylist who could follow her. She first tried Garnett Clark, and then found a man whom Mae Barnes believes was "the only man I think she ever loved in her life."[2] His name was Bobby Henderson, a talented pianist whose interpretation of current hits had gained him a following of his own. Henderson was also a thoughtful and observant man who lived with his mother. He had given up his studies to become a bookkeeper to try his luck at becoming a jazz musician. He first saw Billie at Pod's and Jerry's and soon began accompanying her during her sets. Away from the club, the two spent more and more time together. "I never met anybody like Billie," Henderson said.[3] Although Billie was special to Henderson, he seems to have realized that the 16-year-old singer was almost too much for him. Although a seasoned jazz musician, Henderson never thought of himself as cool, unlike Billie, who once described herself as "a hip kitty."[4] Even though he was five years older, Henderson was struck by how worldly Billie was and that, in fact, she had seen and experienced more by age 16 than most other girls.

Still, Henderson loved the way she dressed, moved, even how she ate. He recalled that she was very graceful, almost dainty, in the way she handled utensils. He also saw Billie's bad side: her terrible temper, her stubbornness, her manipulation of others. But her skills as a singer were unquestionable; her timing was impeccable and even though Billie was at the beginning of her career, Henderson recognized that she had the talent to become a top vocalist.

At some point, the two became engaged. Henderson took Billie home to meet his mother. Unlike Billie's relationship with Sadie, Henderson and his mother were close; she was supportive of his career and always welcomed his friends to her home. Billie reciprocated the gesture, though by the time Henderson visited, relations between Billie and her mother were strained. Henderson recalled that during his visit the two did nothing but yell at each other. It was a pattern often repeated during Henderson's relationship with Billie. At times, Henderson intervened, talking to both women in an attempt to cool tempers. But he also found himself having to defend Billie during work or after hours. Although Henderson could take care of himself and protect Billie, Billie herself never shied away from a fight. Henderson was not used to such behavior, especially from women. Her actions toward Sadie and her tough attitudes more than likely contributed to Henderson's decision not to pursue the relationship.

It was becoming painfully clear to Henderson that he was not the man for Billie, nor she the woman for him. Billie gravitated toward men who were tough and hard, men whom she could fight with, and then reject, just as she was rejected throughout her childhood and young adulthood. Henderson was a gentler soul. Eventually the couple drifted apart; on December 1, 1934, *New York Age* announced, "Bobby Henderson, pianist, no longer engaged to Billie Holiday."[5]

A FAST LIFE

Despite growing praise for her singing, those who watched and worked with Holiday began to notice some disturbing, even destructive, behavior. She loved the fast life, and although she made good money working the "bar-and-grill" circuit, she rarely hung on to it. She instead spent it on liquor, drugs, clothing, the movies, and vaudeville shows. Eating and sleeping were afterthoughts. Billie was constantly on the go, racing from job to job, and afterward to clubs or parties.

When Billie drank too much or smoked too much marijuana, she became even more belligerent. Pop Foster, an entertainer and comedian, remembers that when she was drunk or high, Billie would "fight at the snap of a finger. She was always trying to have some fun, but if anybody crossed her she was really bad. We used to smoke a lot of pot together.... She was quiet ... unless somebody flustered her ... [then] she'd raise hell."[6]

It was clear that Billie was having the time of her life and was probably happier than she had ever been. She did not care that her career had no direction or that she was a relative unknown. Others saw her differently; as Willie "the Lion" Smith stated, Billie was good, but talent was not everything. Already, she was drinking too much; that, along with her bad temper, had already gotten her fired from several singing jobs.

"I HAD FOUND A STAR"

Along the bumpy road of finding work as a singer, Billie began to make some important friends. While working at Mexico's, she met an enterprising songwriter named Bernie Hanighen. While at Harvard, Hanighen had written several musicals as well as forming his own jazz band. After graduating, he moved to New York to try to break into the music business. Because of his talent and previous experience, Hanighen already had established contacts, including John Hammond.

Hanighen demonstrated several of his songs for Billie. One, "If the Moon Turns Green," caught her fancy, and she began to sing it at many of her engagements. Another Hanighen tune, "When a Woman Loves a Man," also became a part of her regular repertoire and a Holiday standard. Excited by Billie's talent and skill, Hanighen later asked her if she would cut a few paper audition discs that he could take around to other bands. Made with a paper base, the discs were among the earliest records made during the 1920s and 1930s. Hanighen's persistence eventually paid off; bandleader Eddie Condon, a young, white Chicago jazz musician, liked what he heard and hired Billie to appear with his band for ten dollars (or approximately 150 dollars in today's currency).

John Hammond had been busy too. Working as an unofficial press agent for Billie, he began writing articles about her singing. In the April 1933 edition of *Melody Maker,* Hammond stated "I had found a star.... Something must be done about her for gramophone records."[7] Hammond also took musicians and others involved in the music industry to hear Billie whenever possible, among them, Joe Glaser, manager for Louis Armstrong; and clarinetist and bandleader Benny Goodman, one of the first white bandleaders to employ African American musicians. Glaser was so impressed by Holiday that he agreed to take her on as a client. Goodman, too, thought enough of Billie's talents that he agreed to take a chance on her and feature her on a record. On the face of it, making a record with Goodman seemed like the big break Billie needed to launch her career.

A NEW AND PROMISING BUSINESS

During the 1930s, the recording industry was still in its infancy; the first RCA Victor Talking Machine Company record player—the Victrola—had only been introduced in 1901. Even though the recording industry grew rapidly, no one thought at first of recording jazz music. That changed in 1915 when a spokesman from the Victor Talking Machine Company approached Creole trumpeter Freddie Keppard and his Original Creole Orchestra about recording their music. Keppard refused, in part because he would not be paid. More important was Keppard's fear that his material would be stolen, stating to his band, "Nothing doing, boys. We won't put our stuff on records for everybody to steal."[8] It was a missed opportunity: in 1917, the all-white Original Dixieland Jazz Band sold more than a million copies of their version of New Orleans jazz, outselling such popular recording artists as opera singer Enrico Caruso and the composer/bandleader John Phillip Sousa.

By the 1920s, records were big business. But even with the growing popularity of African American bands and music, record producers still balked when it came to recording them, arguing that white audiences would be more inclined to buy jazz recordings made by white musicians. Instead, other record labels began offering recordings known as "race records," that is, recordings aimed at specific groups, such as African Americans, or immigrant groups, such as the Jews, Italians, or Poles. By 1917, record companies such as Okeh, Paramount, Vocalion, and Columbia began to market "race records" for African Americans. These recordings allowed many African American artists to reach a national audience for the first time. Black record producer Perry Bradford explained in 1920, "There's 14 million Negroes in our great country and they will buy records if recorded by one of their own, because we are the only folks that can sing and interpret hot jazz songs just off the griddle."[9]

Eventually, white record producers recognized they were not only losing prospective customers but potential dollars too. These record companies, however, had restrictive ideas about selling music, and so they decided what type of music was appropriate for each audience. For white bands, it was best to stick to sweet and sentimental tunes. For African American musicians, blues and other types of Southern black music worked best, supposedly because this music came naturally to, and would be bought by, African Americans only.

As with many other businesses, the recording industry had been hit hard by the Depression. People had no money to spend on things like records; as a result, sales plunged. After selling more than 100 million records a year in the mid-1920s, record company sales dropped to 6 million during the early years of the Depression. Many record companies had gone out of business; others, such as the RCA Victor Talking Machine Company, stopped making record players altogether for a time and sold radios instead. Instead of playing records, people now burned them as fuel. However, where many saw an industry heading for disaster, others, such as John Hammond, saw only opportunity.

FIRST TRY

To produce Billie's first record, Hammond turned to the struggling American Columbia. Even though the company was on the verge of bankruptcy, Hammond had come up with a plan in which the company could import titles from its British counterpart, English Columbia. The company, though selling to an English audience, often set up its own recording sessions in the United States. This way, Hammond could not only record American artists, but also have a ready-made market, as English audiences generally were far more interested in American jazz than were Americans. It did not hurt that the Depression had not hit England.

Besides the Garland Wilson recordings, by 1933, Hammond set up record deals with the Benny Carter Orchestra, Fletcher Henderson's Orchestra, and Benny Goodman's band. In just two months, Hammond had recorded 14 sessions and had achieved some success. It was an important move, for it established Hammond as a music producer to be reckoned with. At the time, Hammond was only 23 years old. With some experience under his belt, Hammond negotiated a recording date for Billie. It wasn't much; Billie was to be squeezed into another recording session, but it was a start.

On November 27, 1933, Billie Holiday entered the Columbia studios located on Fifth Avenue in New York City. Thanks to Hammond and Benny Goodman, nine musicians from Goodman's band would accompany her. For both men, the recording session marked an important turning point in jazz history, particularly for women vocalists. Not only would the session feature the debut of Billie Holiday, it also was the last recording session for one of the greatest female blues singers of all time, Ethel Waters.

Waters, most likely born in 1896, is credited with bringing black urban blues to white audiences. Born because of the rape of her 12-year-old mother by a white man, John Waters, Ethel was raised by her maternal grandmother. Performing was in Waters's blood. Her first performance was at the age of five where she sang as Baby Star in a children's church program. Waters left home and school at the age of 13 in order to support herself by working as a domestic. She later began performing on

the black vaudeville circuit and became known as Sweet Mama Stringbean. In 1919, Waters moved to New York City; with the advent of the
Harlem Renaissance, Waters's singing talent landed her recording jobs at
the African American company Black Swan Records and later Columbia Records. By refining the lyrics and her performance, Waters created a
niche for the black nightclub singers, such as Billie Holiday, who gained
popularity between the 1930s and the 1950s.

Billie was nervous when she arrived at the studio. Although she considered herself a seasoned performer, all of her singing had been done live.
Recording was a very different undertaking. When she learned she would
have to sing into a large microphone, Billie's anxiety increased, and she
pleaded with Hammond not to make her do so. The presence of Ethel
Waters in the studio only escalated Billie's case of nerves. Even though
Waters said she was there to listen, it was obvious that she also wanted to
check out Hammond's discovery.

As if she did not already have enough to contend with, there was the
matter of the song Billie was slated to sing. "Your Mother's Son-in-Law"
was in a key that Billie found uncomfortable, and Goodman, who liked
to drive the beat, wanted her to pick up the tempo. The band did several
run-throughs until Billie was ready to step to the microphone. Despite her
fears, Billie recorded the song in three takes. Before she knew it, she was
done. She collected her thirty-five dollars for the session and headed home,
unimpressed with the experience and disappointed in her performance.

Billie's reservations notwithstanding, her singing during the session
was much better than she thought. Despite the uncomfortable key and
tempo, it was obvious to Hammond that her first effort was good enough
to get her back into the studio to try again. On December 4, Billie arrived again at Columbia studios to record another song with Goodman,
"Riffin' the Scotch," written expressly with Billie in mind. However, the
original lyrics, written by Goodman's guitarist, Dick McDonough, did not
quite work. McDonough sought the help of Johnny Mercer, a young songwriter and lyricist from Georgia. Mercer's revisions aided the evolution of
Billie's style. She not only incorporated Louis Armstrong's improvisation
and Bessie Smith's economy of style, but now also added what became one
of her greatest themes of her career: a woman unlucky in love.

This element was already popular among "torch singers." Usually white
and female, torch singers sang sentimental songs of unrequited or lost love.
The term came from the saying that someone was "carrying a torch," or longing, for a lost love. Sung in sultry and sensual tones, these songs figuratively
resembled a smoldering torch. During the 1920s and 1930s, there were a
number of popular torch singers, including the French singer Édith Piaf, the

German actress Marlene Dietrich, and Ethel Waters. Mercer thought that Billie's voice possessed the same qualities as the leading torch singers and strove to accent them in reworking McDonough's "Riffin' the Scotch."

Nevertheless, the session did not go well; the two recordings that Billie did were discarded. Billie blamed the arranger. Hammond, though, did not give up. On December 18, he brought Billie back in to the studio. This time, her rendition of "Riffin' the Scotch" was deemed good enough to be included on a record that featured solos by Charles Teagarden and Shirley Clay, two popular singers of the day. Taken with her earlier effort, "Your Mother's Son-in Law," "Riffin' the Scotch" went a long way toward establishing Billie's style. In only three years, between 1930 and 1933, Billie created her signature style. At the time of the December 1933 sessions, she was only 18 years old.

BACK TO BASICS

By 1934, Billie's career was gaining momentum. Hammond wrote about her at every opportunity. Yet, record sales were disappointing. Billie also faced mounting competition from young female singers who wanted a chance to perform in Harlem's many clubs. In late 1934, Billie and Bobby Henderson, who would end their relationship in less than a month, received an invitation to perform at the Apollo Theater. Although many thought Henderson's piano playing rather than Billie's singing got them the slot, it was still a big break for both. On November 23, 1934, the duo of Henderson and Halliday (as Billie's name was spelled on the marquee) made their debut. The appearance was disappointing and received no critical notice.

By 1935, her romance with Henderson at an end, Billie paid greater attention to her career. She lined up as many jobs as she could, appearing at the Hot-Cha and the Sunset clubs. Columnists began paying closer critical attention to her; soon her name began appearing more often in the entertainment columns. Not all the reviews were favorable. After one of her performances at the Sunset, Billie insulted entertainment writer Marcus Wright of *New York Age*. Wright returned the compliment in his next column, writing:

> Billie Halliday [sic] when you think you are playing sophisticated, take a look in the mirror before you make your appearance at the Hot-Cha, then you will find out you are not so hot after all, you are just an entertainer.[10]

Contrary to Wright's snipings, Billie was becoming a poised and sophisticated performer who delighted audiences and who was now coming to the attention of the music world.

SYMPHONY IN BLACK

In 1934, John Hammond was working at the offices of one of New York City's top show business impresarios, Irving Mills. Mills managed some of the biggest names in jazz, including Duke Ellington and Cab Calloway. Acting on Billie's behalf, Hammond told Mills that she was a star on the rise in need of guidance and sound representation. Hammond's efforts paid off; after hearing Billie, Mills agreed to take her on as a client. One of his first efforts to raise Billie's profile was to have her featured in a short film called *Symphony in Black,* which showcased Ellington's band. A little more than nine minutes long, *Symphony in Black* took more than 10 months to complete. Ellington chose the music carefully to make sure it fit Billie's style. Having Billie sing "Saddest Tale," a song about a woman jilted by her man, was an astute move on Ellington's part. Her performance was mesmerizing. When released in September 1935, *Symphony in Black* was a hit.

Symphony in Black marked an important milestone in the development of Billie Holiday, the woman and the singer. Ellington's deft handling enabled Billie to distinguish herself from other torch singers. She did not wear her emotions on her sleeve; instead, she revealed herself gradually as the song unfolded. Hers was a carefully crafted and sophisticated performance, especially for a woman only 19 years old. This carefully woven tapestry of life and music was the origin of the persona that audiences came to identify with Billie. Other singers such as Frank Sinatra and Judy Garland may have more successfully established and cultivated an image, but Billie Holiday did it first.

NOTES

1. John Hammond and Irving Townsend, *John Hammond on Record* (London: Penguin, 1981), p. 92.

2. Donald Clarke, *Wishing on the Moon: The Life and Times of Billie Holiday* (New York: Viking, 1994), p. 51.

3. Ibid., p. 59.

4. Billie Holiday, with William Dufty, *Lady Sings the Blues* (New York: Penguin, 1992), p. 20.

5. Clarke, *Wishing on the Moon,* p. 64.

6. Julia Blackburn, *With Billie* (New York: Pantheon, 2005), p. 78.

7. Hammond and Townsend, *John Hammond on Record,* p. 93.

8. Ken Burns, "Race Records," PBS series "Jazz," 2001, http://www.pbs.org/jazz/exchange/exchange_race_records.htm.

9. Ibid.

10. Marcus Wright, *New York Age,* December 29, 1934, p. 9.

Chapter 4

A RISING STAR

By February 1935, Billie Holiday was making a name for herself. After her screen debut in *Symphony in Black*, her manager, Irving Mills, was anxious to keep the momentum going. He offered her a try-out with the Mills Blue Rhythm Band at the Lincoln Theater in Philadelphia. The band, recently put under contract by Mills, was used mainly to fill in bookings when Mills's two biggest stars, Duke Ellington and Cab Calloway, were playing other engagements. However, the Blues Rhythm Band was no slouch either; many dancers and singers considered the group to be one of the top jazz bands. A dispute with the management of the theater, though, quickly ended Billie's chance to perform, yet another setback in Billie's quest to become a star.

A FUTURE EMPLOYER

Ralph Cooper should have been a content man. Between 1932 and 1935, he had worked hard to become the leader of the best band in Harlem. Cooper and his band, the Kongo Knights, became so popular that in 1934 he became emcee (or master of ceremonies) at the famous Apollo Theater.

Established in 1913 at 253 West 125th Street in Harlem, the Apollo was the central theater. Initially the venue for burlesque shows, in which comics, dancers, singers, and other assorted acts performed. The Apollo later staged musical revues, which featured many of the top jazz bands and singers of the day. African Americans were first allowed to attend performances at the Apollo in January 1934, around the same time that

Ralph Cooper began as the master of ceremonies. That year also brought the creation of the weekly talent show called Amateur Night. Held on Wednesdays, these shows featured many of the performers who became legendary in jazz, rhythm and blues, and rock and roll. Ella Fitzgerald, Lena Horne, Sam Cooke, Marvin Gaye, and James Brown first came to public notice when they took the stage during one of the Amateur Nights at the Apollo. Those who performed played to a tough crowd, for it was generally acknowledged that the Apollo audiences were sophisticated, discerning, and critical. Success at the Apollo launched the careers of many African American entertainers.

SPAGHETTI WITH A SONG

Despite his growing celebrity, Ralph Cooper missed leading the Kongo Knights. By the end of March 1935, he was busy assembling another band that included some of the best talent available, such as saxophonists Louis Jordan and Emmett Mathews. Cooper's stature enabled him to schedule the band's debut at the Apollo in April. Even before the first performance, "Ralph Cooper with his 18 Kings of Melody" was a sensation.

Just days before the Kings of Melody were to appear on the Apollo stage, Cooper dined at one of his favorite restaurants, the Hot-Cha, where he ordered spaghetti. Cooper paid no attention to the young woman who was preparing to sing. Singers were a dime a dozen in Harlem; one was as good—or as bad—as the next.

Once the singer began, however, Cooper took immediate notice. She had a voice like no one else. Her singing, he recalled, sounded just like a woman crying. Cooper knew talent when he saw and heard it. As soon as the singer finished, he rushed to the stage and asked if she would consider being the vocalist for his new band.

Billie was thrilled. She knew Cooper's reputation as one of the leading bandleaders in Harlem. She agreed without hesitation, and Cooper immediately negotiated with Billie's boss for her release from her current contract. He told Billie to come for rehearsals the day of the band's Apollo performance. After experiencing so many ups and downs in her brief career, Billie hoped that Cooper's offer was the big break she needed.

Yet, when Billie arrived at the theater to start rehearsals, things went badly from the start. She did not have an appropriate stage costume and had to find something suitable to wear. Her rehearsals with the band went poorly, and many of the musicians believed she could not handle the material. Cooper held firm, convinced that when the time came, Billie would hold her own on stage.

Dressed in a cheap white satin gown, Billie watched from the wings as the Kings of Melody opened the show. When she heard the band playing her opening tune, Billie had an attack of stage fright. When she started to walk away, an old-time performer, comedian Pigmeat Markham, grabbed her by the shoulders and pushed her onto the stage. Billie described what happened next:

> My knees was shaking so bad the people didn't know whether I was going to dance or sing. Even after I opened my mouth they weren't sure. One little broad in the front row hollered out, "Look she's dancing and singing at the same time."[1]

The critics were equally unimpressed. One suggested that Holiday's style did not fit with that of Cooper's band. But despite this lukewarm reception, the Kings of Melody, featuring Billie Holiday, were held over at the Apollo for another week.

Cooper made the most of the opportunity. He substituted several up-tempo numbers for the slow, sad songs that Billie had sung in her first performance. Yet, he decided to take no chances and brought in Herb Jeffries, a popular jazz singer from Chicago, just in case Billie failed. Cooper's hunches paid off, Jeffries was a huge hit, and Billie fared better with her new repertoire.

But Billie's moment ended before it really got started. Cooper's popularity as Apollo emcee made it impossible to devote himself to leading a band. When the Kings of Melody completed the Apollo engagement, Cooper dissolved the band, and Billie returned to singing at the Hot-Cha.

By now, Billie was becoming frustrated and depressed over the direction of her career. Although she had sung in some of Harlem's biggest clubs, Billie felt that she would never get her big break. To make matters worse, there was a new female singer who was getting rave notices from critics and musicians alike. At 18 years old, she already had landed a job with the Chick Webb Orchestra, one of the hottest bands in town. Her name was Ella Fitzgerald.

Curious and jealous, Billie went to see Fitzgerald perform. One musician recalled how Billie swept into the Savoy and glared at Fitzgerald, her anger obvious to all around her. Billie did not understand why Fitzgerald was getting the better jobs than she. A seasoned veteran at the age of 20, Billie toiled on for the bar-and-grill circuit. Her career, it seemed, had stalled, and her prospects were diminishing. She received better news in June 1935. John Hammond, still championing Billie's singing, had arranged a deal with Brunswick Records to get Billie back into the studio, accompanied by the noted jazz pianist Teddy Wilson.

TEDDY WILSON

Born on November 24, 1911, in Tuskegee, Alabama, Wilson studied piano at nearby Talladega College. Among his first professional experiences was playing with Louis Armstrong. In 1933, Wilson moved to New York City, where he joined Benny Carter's band, the "Chocolate Dandies," and began his recording career. In 1935 he met Benny Goodman; he later joined Goodman's band, making Goodman's outfit the first integrated jazz band.

Wilson modeled his playing on the style of Earl "Fatha" Hines, one of the first great jazz pianists. Hines's distinctive "trumpet" style, so called because of his frequent use of single-note phrases and *arpeggios* (fast successions of notes in a chord) that resembled jazz brass players, was imitated by a whole generation of up-and-coming jazz pianists. Wilson later forged his own unique approach from Hines's influence, becoming an accomplished jazz pianist known for his restrained, dignified, and elegant playing.

Not only did Hammond have Wilson on board, but, as producer, he had his pick of the top musicians available, including clarinetist Benny Goodman, trumpet player Roy Eldridge, and saxophonist Ben Webster. Still, it was the Depression and money was tight; in order to pay his musicians, Hammond had to forego buying arrangements for Billie's songs. To help, Wilson agreed to sketch out arrangements. Wilson did not write all the parts of the song; rather, he outlined the introduction and ending of the songs and noted the basic harmonies that the musicians would play.

Holiday was no stranger to Wilson; he and his wife had caught Billie when she was singing at a club on Seventh Avenue. Wilson's wife, Irene, later recalled that Billie, dressed in a lavender skirt with a pink top, looked more like an overgrown child than a young woman. But when Billie came to the Wilsons' house to rehearse, he discovered a talented young singer who needed direction and help honing her style. The day before the recording session, Wilson selected the songs and ran through them with Billie. Wilson's input was vital, as Billie focused on her phrasing and interpretation. For the next several months, Wilson and Holiday worked together; with Wilson arranging her material, Holiday took another step in developing her style.

1776 BROADWAY

On July 2,1935, at the Brunswick Studios, John Hammond, Teddy Wilson, and other members of the band met with Billie Holiday to begin recording for the Columbia label. As Hammond wanted the session to be as relaxed as possible, he arranged to have the group meet in the late afternoon. The sessions almost did not go; that day Hammond learned that Benny Goodman was scheduled to play out of town that weekend, and had called for a rehearsal of his own band. Hammond got on the phone and angrily demanded that Goodman honor his first commitment. Whatever Hammond said, it worked; less than 10 minutes after their conversation, Goodman was at the studio, ready to go, with the understanding that he could leave early to keep his other commitment. The session was a lively one, possibly inspired by Goodman's need to meet his other band for rehearsal. Whatever the reason, the session turned out to be one of the most remarkable in jazz history.

During the next four years, from 1935 to 1939, Holiday stepped into the studio several more times. The recordings that emerged from these sessions are still considered to be among her best. Although labeled a blues singer, Holiday's catalogue during this period includes only two real blues numbers: "Billie's Blues," recorded in 1936, and "Long Gone Blues," in 1939. Many of the other songs came from the pens of popular songwriters, including "I Cried for You," "I Must Have That Man," "Who Loves You," "Them There Eyes," and "The Man I Love." As a friend once remarked, "She liked difficult songs, songs with something to them."[2] In her singing, Holiday transformed many songs, sometimes happy, songs, into music that had an extra dimension, filled with soul and emotion that made them uniquely her own.

MISSTEPS

In September 1935, two months after her first Brunswick recording session, Holiday accepted an engagement at New York's Famous Door, a club owned by a group of white musicians that included Jimmy Dorsey. Holiday and Teddy Wilson were booked to open for the featured attraction, a Dixieland group led by trombonist George Brunis. The pairing was a disaster. Known for an unsophisticated and sometimes crude brand of musical clowning, Brunis attracted an audience that found his antics appealing. In addition, Brunis's attitude toward his supporting act was racist and demeaning. For Teddy Wilson, surviving the engagement became a matter of fading into the background and keeping to himself. Holiday took the opposite approach and took Brunis head-on, complaining about her treatment. Brunis ignored her and continued to do what he could to make Holiday as uncomfortable as possible, informing her that she was not allowed to mingle with the guests between sets or sit at the bar; during her rest periods, she was forced to hang around outside the patrons' toilets. After four days, the engagement was terminated by mutual consent of both parties.

At the end of 1935, Billie formed a business association with Joe Glaser, a prominent New York talent agent. The son of a wealthy and proper Chicago family, Glaser had spent most of his life around music and musicians. His interests were both legal and illegal; he owned an automobile agency, had an interest in prizefighters, and was rumored to own a house of prostitution. A brush with the law in 1933 convinced the young Glaser that it was time to move on.

He arrived in New York City later that year and quickly began making a name for himself, working at the powerful Rockwell-O'Keefe Agency. A shrewd man and a bit of a roughneck, Glaser realized that there were no professional artists' managers who specialized in black talent, and he decided to fill the void. He also decided to build the biggest agency that represented African American performers. Because of his genuine concern for and loyalty to the people he handled, Glaser counted some of the biggest African American talents among his clients, including Count Basie and Louis Armstrong.

One of Glaser's first efforts came in early in 1936 when he got Holiday a spot in a musical revue at Connie's Inn, where she made a hit singing "You Let Me Down." Soon after opening, Holiday became ill and was replaced by the great blues singer Bessie Smith. It also became clear that Holiday was ill suited for the over-the-top musical delivery that people expected at these extravaganzas. Hoping to win her job back, Holiday was disappointed again when the management decided to keep Bessie Smith on permanently.

Holiday's mishaps continued. Glaser asked Ed Fox, manager of the Grand Terrace Ballroom in Chicago, to feature Holiday with the Fletcher Henderson band. Upon hearing the news, Holiday was ecstatic; Henderson's band comprised some of the best jazz musicians, many of whom were personal friends of hers.

However, the engagement turned into another debacle. Holiday found Fox to be coarse and crude, viewing performers as commodities with little regard for their talent. Fox also took an immediate dislike to Holiday, berating her in public. It took only two nights of Fox's continual haranguing before Holiday had enough; the two engaged in a yelling and screaming match with Holiday smashing furniture and throwing a glass inkwell at Fox's head. Within days, she was on the train back to New York with no paycheck. Hurt by the band's unwillingness to stand up for her and to take on Fox, Holiday got an even ruder surprise from Glaser, who told her that she should have just stuck it out. His comment led to another angry confrontation, but neither held grudges, and shortly Glaser again began lining up work for Holiday. Years later when asked about her experience in Chicago, Holiday replied, "They run me out of Chicago.... Ed Fox ... he say, 'What the hell ... you stink my ... show up! Everybody says you sing too slow. Get out!'"[3]

In September 1936, Glaser booked Holiday to perform at the Onyx Club in New York City, where she sang during the intermissions in the show of the main attraction, jazz violinist Stuff Smith and his Sextet. A bill of Holiday and Smith seemed an inspired combination, until Holiday's performance wowed audiences. Smith became so enraged that he threatened to quit unless management fired Holiday. In the end, Smith got his way. For Holiday, the incident was another piece of bad luck.

SOME GOOD NEWS

Holiday may not have been making progress as a live performer, but her recording career blossomed. By the late 1930s, she recorded regularly for Columbia, usually under the direction of Teddy Wilson, with a small studio band made up of the best jazz musicians of the day. In general, the recordings were intended for a black audience and consisted of silly and second-rate love songs that white singers had declined to record. But with Wilson's thoughtful arrangements, Holiday turned these otherwise forgettable songs into jazz classics. While not immediately appreciated by casual listeners, Holiday was gaining more of a reputation among musicians, critics, and hard-core jazz fans. With Teddy Wilson, Holiday recorded some 100 songs that today are considered among her most significant work.

By 1936, Billie's recordings enjoyed a modest success, selling steadily, if not spectacularly, both in the United States and in Europe. Sales were encouraging enough that American Record Company decided to record Holiday again. At this point, Holiday cared little whether she received royalties; more important was having her name featured on the label.

To help her with the upcoming studio sessions, John Hammond brought in a new producer, a young Harvard-educated man from Nebraska, Bernie Hanighen. Hanighen had already enjoyed some fame of his own as collaborator with lyricist Johnny Mercer on a number of songs, many of which are considered among the best in Mercer's catalogue.

In late June 1936, Billie was back in the studio with Hammond and Hanighen. This time around, Holiday's recording sessions and musical selections were far better than those she had done with Teddy Wilson. Under Hanighen's guidance, Holiday cut four good songs. In September, Hanighen had Holiday back in the studio, working the same magic.

By now, Holiday's material was improving as songwriters slowly became convinced that her unconventional singing style could sell records. It seemed, finally, that the pieces were falling into place.

Billie's live performances also took a more hopeful turn. The Onyx Club owner Joe Helbock, who had fired Holiday because of Stuff Smith, still felt bad about dismissing her. At the earliest opportunity, Helbock brought Holiday back to the Onyx Club. Her successful appearance raised her confidence, and not long afterward, she was booked at the Uptown House in Harlem, where she had another long and favorable engagement.

As she gained experience, Holiday began to groom herself to look the part of a sophisticated and glamorous young woman. She marceled her hair, a popular hairstyle that involved using a curling iron to impress the hair with deep, regular waves. She powdered her face, which also featured highly arched and penciled eyebrows, and carefully applied lipstick. Her clothing became more urbane as well: long gowns, accented by pearl necklaces draped around her neck and hoop earrings, replaced the cheap satin dresses. She cultivated a look very different from that of other cabaret and club singers and dancers, who went for a more exotic appearance, dressing in costumes so daring and risqué as to evoke stereotypical images of African savages. Holiday instead wanted a look that was groomed and elegant; she did not hide her sexuality but did not exploit either. It was another way in which she was distanced herself from other female singers.

ANOTHER DISCOVERY

At the same time Billie was working at the Uptown, John Hammond was traveling west in search of new talent. While driving south of Chicago, he happened to catch on the radio a Kansas City broadcast featuring the music of New Jersey–born William "Count" Basie. Hammond was no stranger to Basie's music, having met him in 1932 at a show in Harlem. After hearing the broadcast, Hammond headed to Kansas City and the Reno Club where the band was playing. There he had the opportunity not only to see Basie, but to check out the other musicians who played with him, particularly a young tenor saxophonist named Lester Young.

MR. LESTER YOUNG

Born in 1909 in Woodville, Mississippi, Lester Young was the eldest of three children. His father, Willis Handy Young, was a versatile carnival musician who taught music to all his children. Eventually, the elder Young formed a family band in which Lester played alto saxophone; the family went on the road playing carnivals and other shows to earn money. In 1927, Lester quit the family group and left to make his own way as a musician; he soon found work playing with jazz groups as a tenor saxophonist.

Young returned home in 1929, but the family decided to move to California. Young left again and this time went to New York, where he was hired as a replacement for the great saxophonist Coleman Hawkins, then playing with Fletcher Henderson's Orchestra. Young's time with the band was brief and disastrous; the other musicians, used to Hawkins's full-bodied style, had little use for a youngster whose playing was decidedly lighter in tone. To make things worse, most of his bandmates questioned Young's abilities as a musician in general, leaving Young, a sensitive and quiet man but with a deep resolve, angry and frustrated. The situation deteriorated further when Henderson's wife, also a musician, offered to help Young with his playing. By now, Young had enough and as quickly as possible obtained his release from Henderson along with a letter stating that his leaving had nothing to do with his talent. Young then headed to Kansas City, where he found work with local area bands. In the summer of 1936, things began looking up for Young when he signed with the Count Basie Band.

A BIG BREAK

Hammond was so enthused about Basie's group that he contacted a young talent agent, Willard Alexander, and persuaded him to represent the band. Not long after, Basie and his band headed east, reaching New York in December 1936. Hammond was busy trying to find ways to enhance the group's dynamic and sound by seeking replacements for one or two of the musicians whose playing was weak. In the midst of his auditioning, he found out that the group had signed a record deal with Decca instead of ARC. Despite this setback, Hammond continued to arrange for a recording session for Holiday that featured Teddy Wilson and members of Basie's band.

Hammond had no idea of what to expect from the session he had arranged. On paper, the makeup of the group seemed a recipe for disaster. The only experienced studio musicians present were Benny Goodman and Teddy Wilson; Hammond was simply hoping the other musicians would hold their own. In January 1937, Holiday, Hammond, and the other musicians gathered in the studio. The project was doomed almost before it began; an ARC executive walked into the room, and smelling the air, noticed that the smoke was not coming from tobacco, but rather from marijuana. Through some clever talking, Hammond convinced him that everything would be fine.

Hammond was right; not only did the session go off well, but the results are considered among the greatest recording sessions in jazz history. Holiday was in fine form and the interplay of her voice with Lester Young's saxophone created the foundation for a professional and personal relationship that lasted until his death. By the end, four songs were in place, including "He Ain't Got Rhythm," "This Year's Kisses," "Why Was I Born," and "I Must Have That Man," which became part of Holiday's repertoire.

For Holiday, life was good; she was gaining greater fame, her recordings were selling respectably, and she had a steady job. She was performing with some of the biggest names in jazz; it was hard to believe that less than three years earlier she had been a struggling cabaret singer. Once again, though, fate stepped in, denying Holiday the chance to enjoy her success; another cruel blow was waiting for her just around the corner.

NOTES

1. Billie Holiday, with William Dufty, *Lady Sings the Blues* (New York: Penguin, 1992), p. 40.

2. Robert O'Meally, *Lady Day: The Many Faces of Billie Holiday* (New York: Little, Brown, 1991), p. 117.

3. *The Complete Billie Holiday on Verve*, 517658–2, Disc 4, track 8.

Chapter 5

ON THE ROAD

On March 1, 1937, while performing at the Uptown, Holiday received a phone call from Dallas. The voice on the other end of the line wanted to know if she was the daughter of a Clarence Holiday. When she said that she was, the caller told her that her father was dead. Holiday was distraught; it was left to Clarke Monroe, the owner of the club, to find out the necessary details about the burial. He also loaned Billie the use of his car so that she and Sadie could go to the funeral.

In the months before his death, Holiday was touring with the Don Redman Band. While traveling in the Southwest, Holiday came down with a bad cold; instead of seeking medical attention, he continued to work. Because of the racial climate of the period, it was difficult for African Americans to receive good medical care. Not only were blacks turned away from doctors' offices, but hospitals either ignored or refused to treat them. As a result, Holiday's cold turned into pneumonia, and he died at the St. Paul Sanitarium in Dallas. He was only 37. The circumstances of his death were not lost on his daughter, who later wrote in her autobiography that "It wasn't the pneumonia that killed him, it was Dallas."[1]

Although Billie and her father were never close, a bond did exist between them. Probably much more than Sadie, Clarence understood his daughter's profession and the kinds of sacrifices she had to make and problems she had to overcome to have any success. Despite the infrequent contact Clarence had with both his daughter and Sadie, the two were not only overcome with grief, but with guilt as well; Billie for the lost opportunities with a father she needed, and Sadie, for failing to maintain a relationship with Clarence.

Compounding the situation was the presence of Clarence's second wife, Fanny Holiday. An argument broke out between Fanny and Sadie over who would ride in the first car, reserved for the family. When Fanny prevailed, Sadie refused to ride with anyone and instead rented her own car; on her way to the cemetery, Sadie got lost, arriving hours after the burial service. It might have been just as well; also attending the service was Clarence's unacknowledged third wife, a white woman who bore two children by him.

Yet, Sadie's grief was real and deep. Writing of her mother and father, Billie said that Clarence was:

> The only man [Sadie] ever really loved. They hadn't been together for years, but that didn't change the way she felt about him. She felt he still belonged to her, or some part of him did, and she never got over his death.[2]

BACK TO WORK

The emotional upheaval of Clarence Holiday's funeral and the time lost to traveling left Holiday out of work and with no prospects in sight. John Hammond once again came to her rescue. His newest find, the Count Basie Band, was struggling in New York. Hammond decided to revamp the makeup of the band. First, he suggested Basie expand his vocal repertoire and hire a new singer; bands with female singers were big business. Hammond had just the singer for Basie: Billie Holiday.

Holiday had some experience as a band singer, but had long since moved on to being featured as a soloist. But she needed the job and was excited about working with Basie again, so she accepted Hammond's offer. She was happy too about her new salary: seventy dollars a week, double what she had been paid working at the Uptown and more than any of the other musicians were making. Even better was the opportunity to reunite with the friends she had made at the 1937 recording session, especially Lester Young, who called her "Lady." Holiday in turn called Young "Pres" since he was the main man, the president.

A DEEP FRIENDSHIP

Billie Holiday's and Lester Young's friendship was an intense, platonic love affair that Holiday nurtured and treasured throughout her lifetime. If anything, Young was often regarded by Holiday as her true soul mate, the one person who truly cared for her and understood her. Together, through their music and personalities, Holiday and Young would emerge as two of the most influential musicians in American jazz history.

The two first met in 1934, when Holiday invited Young to the house she shared with Sadie. Having been in New York only a short time, Young was more than happy to abandon his cheap living arrangements to come and live with the two. Not only did it allow him the opportunity to get to know the city, the arrangement provided Billie the opportunity to work with a musician who was rapidly making a name for himself. The two had many conversations about music; sometimes Billie would sing along with Young, and other times she accompanied him to clubs to watch. Perhaps one of Young's greatest gifts to Holiday was his willingness to share his talent and knowledge. In the end, Holiday became a better singer for it.

Together with Coleman Hawkins, Young was one of the most influential saxophonists of the swing era. His light, airy sound and the melodic grace of his improvisations were a strong contrast to Hawkins's gruffer, more harmonically based approach. Young's velvety tone and rapid articulation were major influences on the bebop generation of saxophonists that followed, notably Charlie Parker. His work with Billie Holiday was nothing short of magical as his delicate phrasing created a subtle counterpoint around Holiday's mesmerizing vocals. To watch the two perform together was to see two artists who not only believed in each other, but through the sheer power of their music communicated on a level not often seen between two musicians.

LIFE ON THE ROAD

Less than two weeks after she buried her father, Holiday was on tour with Count Basie. Their first stop was Scranton, Pennsylvania, where initial reviews of the band and its new singer were quite favorable. Then it was on to the Apollo, where many of her fans greeted Holiday and the band with great enthusiasm. Basie recalled that the applause was so great for Holiday, she had trouble getting off the stage. The band then moved on to the Savoy, where again audiences showered their applause on both Basie and Billie Holiday. By this time, Basie had developed a deep respect and affection for his singer. He later told an interviewer that he and Holiday "were tight.... I loved Billie an awful lot. I loved her as far as love could go."[3]

On stage, Holiday was unstoppable. Her only request was that she not be asked to sing popular tunes; rather she would sing the material that she believed was better suited to her style. In an interview, Basie described the dynamic between his singer and his musicians: "She fitted in so easily, it was like having another soloist. All she needed was the routine, then she could come in with her eyes closed—no cues or signals."[4] Basie also remembered the almost telepathic way in which Lester Young and Buck Clayton picked up the accompaniment in a way that invariably complemented Billie's voice and phrasing.[5] In his autobiography, Clayton explained, "I would watch her mouth, and when I saw that she was going to take a breath or something I knew it was time for me to play between her expressions. It's what we call 'filling up the windows'."[6]

Working with Basie's band brought a new confidence and vitality to Holiday's singing that she never again experienced. Playing with some of the best jazz musicians in the world allowed her the freedom to experiment with melodies and lyrics. Many consider her time with Basie to be the most creative and rewarding in her life. Between recording sessions and performing with the band, Holiday was not only increasing her public exposure, she was also enjoying more attention from the critics.

The camaraderie on the road between Holiday and the band did not disguise the difficult conditions under which they traveled. Life on the road during the Depression was tough on any band; for a female singer, it often proved to be nightmarish. African American bands found the conditions even harder; for Holiday, touring became a living hell. The hours were irregular; unsanitary conditions and a lack of privacy were continual problems. The band often traveled in shoddy transportation over roads that were in poor condition.

There was also the problem of accommodations. Finding a hotel that would let rooms to African Americans was difficult and, in some places, impossible. Whenever he could, Basie rented apartments for the band; not only did having private living quarters offer a chance for the band members to unwind, it also allowed them to cook their own meals. Although everyone pitched in, it was generally acknowledged that Holiday was the best cook. When accommodations could not be found, the band members slept in their cars.

TROUBLE BREWING

The good relations between Holiday and Basie became severely tested the longer the tour went on. As she had done at her other jobs, Holiday began complaining, if not about working conditions then about her salary. She soon learned that her salary was also to cover the costs of her gowns as well as having her hair done. On top of that, she was already paying for her share of the food and drinks and sending a weekly allowance to her mother. After she had paid her expenses, she often was broke. One friend remembered that when she was in New York, she stopped in at the Hickory House, one of the clubs where she used to perform. She was broke, hungry, and had only enough money to pay for subway fare. One of the musicians bought her a steak dinner; she never forgot that small kindness and years later when the two met in the recording studio, she reminded him of how he had helped her. Despite the problems, though, Holiday was relatively happy; she was performing with an up-and-coming band; she was among close friends; and now she was gaining even wider attention with her performances. For the first time, she felt that she belonged. But as with so many things in her life, her happy situation was destined not to last. After performing with Basie for almost a year, Holiday was fired in 1938.

The reasons for Holiday's dismissal from the Basie band have never been entirely clear. In addition to her complaining, she had become somewhat unreliable. But according to musicians who were aware of the situation, the reasons for Holiday's dismissal were more disturbing. According to music critic Michael Brooks, a prominent figure in the New York publishing industry had a great interest in the Basie band, particularly in Billie Holiday. This individual had influence with many of the prominent club owners as well as some radio stations. He may have also had a financial stake in Basie's band that gave him leverage over Basie. Though the official story was that Holiday was fired for being temperamental and unreliable, the real reason seems to have been her unwillingness to sing female blues songs from the 1920s.[7]

Basie's repertoire consisted mainly of both old and new jazz instrumental numbers. When he used two vocalists, Jimmy Rushing and Holiday, Rushing sang the blues numbers while Holiday handled the pop standards. Ignoring the success of Holiday's recordings, Basie's shadow partner wanted Holiday to revive the 1920s blues numbers that had been made popular by other female blues singers such as Ethel Waters. When Basie suggested the change to Holiday, her response was blunt and clear: she would not sing the older blues standards and would continue to choose songs that were more contemporary. Basie then fired her. After the bad feelings between the two had ebbed, Holiday went to Basie again and asked for a job. Basie replied that he could do nothing, and Holiday was once again out of work. Holiday felt that Basie had betrayed her. She had little money and no immediate prospects. Holiday, though, did not have to wait long for her next job; only a month after Basie fired her, she landed a job with Artie Shaw's big band.

During the 1930s and 1940s, big bands, large musical ensembles that played jazz, were extremely popular. The term emerged out of the musical period known as the Swing Era (1935–1946). Swing has been around since the late 1920s. Most jazz historians, however, believe that the Swing Era began with clarinetist Benny Goodman's performance at the Palomar Ballroom in Los Angeles on August 21, 1935, which was broadcast throughout the country. The Swing Era boasted some of the greatest American musical talent ever, including the Dorsey Brothers, Glenn Miller, Count Basie, Duke Ellington, and Artie Shaw.

Singing with Shaw's band was a big step for Holiday as Shaw was already an established and popular bandleader. Working for him meant better jobs and greater exposure. But Holiday's new opportunity brought with it a new set of problems that eventually ended another friendship.

A NEW ASSOCIATION

By 1938, Artie Shaw was among the most successful big band leaders of the era. By then, big bands had become big business, and it was necessary to come up with a signature style to set one's group off from another. Shaw was known as an innovator among big band leaders, especially when it came to using unusual instrumentation. He is credited with establishing a musical style known as "third stream," that is, the synthesis, or fusion, of classical music and jazz. At the height of his popularity, Shaw reportedly earned thirty thousand dollars per week (approximately four hundred thousand dollars in today's money) and had a string of popular hits such as "Begin the Beguine," "Stardust," and "Frenesi."

At the time he hired her, Shaw was no stranger to Holiday's singing. In a later radio interview, Shaw talked about his initial encounters with her:

> I knew Billie Holiday from my years around Harlem, when I was learning my own trade, when I would sit in with Willie "the Lion" Smith and guys like that and sit in with all the bands, Chick Webb and all these fellas. They were friends of mine and Billie was kidding around singing, and I said to her one time, "some day I'm gonna have a band, [and] you're gonna sing in it." She said, "Yeah, that'll be the day."[8]

Shaw also recalled how he came to hire Holiday; in the spring of 1938, in the midst of a tour, Shaw was still looking for a suitable singer for the band. While working in Boston, he heard that Holiday was back in New York City and out of a job. One evening, late, Shaw drove to Harlem to see her. When the two met, Shaw said, "Come on, you're gonna join my band," to which Holiday scoffed.[9] Shaw then told her to get dressed and gather her things, because she had a job waiting for her in Boston. Upon their arrival, the two rehearsed some of the songs for the next evening's engagement and that was it: Holiday was now part of the Artie Shaw Band. Although Shaw always believed that Holiday would be a tremendous asset to the tour, he had persuaded her to join his big band at a time when a black singer in a white band was shocking. He was not blind to the consequences that awaited them both. Shaw was no stranger to bigotry or racism, having been raised Jewish, and he possessed a keen and sensitive mind. "I knew that was going to be kind of scandalous, but she was a good singer," he said later.[10]

Some Holiday biographers have mistakenly stated that Shaw was the first white bandleader to hire a full-time black female singer. This was not true; a few white bandleaders such as Tommy Dorsey had used black female vocalists in their bands. The difference was that bandleaders such as Dorsey toured exclusively in the North, usually staying in and around New York City, where the racial climate was more tolerant. Shaw was the first to hire a black female singer to tour with an integrated band in the segregated South.

In the late 1930s, big bands competed to play at the most prestigious clubs and ballrooms, with the ultimate goal of landing a network radio show. The music publishers and songwriters played a vital part in this battle, with the best material going to their favorite artists. In March, while still in Boston, Holiday and the band had lined up weekly radio spots that broadcast coast to coast, which gave them a chance to broaden their popular appeal. By April, the band was playing live twice a week on the radio. For Holiday, radio was a godsend; she received good reviews that helped her with future bookings. Critics were also happy with her association with Shaw, stating that her addition to the band meant that Shaw was headed for even bigger successes.

HOSTILE WATERS

As she had with Basie, Holiday refused to sing popular standards with Shaw's band. For the most part, that was fine with him; known as a maverick, Shaw tended to stay away from material that was lightweight, silly, and with little musical merit. He shunned the song pluggers whose job was to advertise new tunes by performing them for bandleaders in the hope that a band or singer would perform them. Shaw was hard enough to deal with, but it was soon apparent that his singer was even worse. There was no way that Billie Holiday would stoop to perform run-of-the-mill material. As *Downbeat* magazine noted in 1938: "She is at her best when she's singing a song she feels deeply and not when she is mouthing inane words to please a song plugger."[11]

Aware that as long as Holiday continued with Shaw's band they had little chance of getting radio play for their songs, some song pluggers began a whispering campaign to discredit Holiday. They believed that if enough pressure were brought to bear on Shaw from management, he would be forced to replace her. No one in the music business was terribly surprised by their efforts; many people were well aware of the lengths to which pluggers would go in order to get their way. Eventually Shaw's manager began leaning hard on his client to find another singer.

Shaw reluctantly agreed and hired a young white singer who performed under the name of Nita Bradley. Holiday performed her own material as a soloist, while Bradley sang popular songs with the band. The two singers did not get along; Holiday for years suspected Bradley of being a racist, which accounted for the tension between them. It did not help either that Holiday often did better with audiences.

Racism only added to Shaw's headaches. He had few illusions, but was still not prepared when the band was turned away from a hotel during a date at a New England college town. When Shaw refused to check in without his band, the management relented and everyone had a room for the night. The band's New England tour had been a good one; not only did they complete a band book of more than 200 arrangements, but the band now enjoyed a greater national following.

After Boston, Shaw arranged for a tour through the South, where he knew the atmosphere would be even less welcoming. Shaw knew Holiday would be a problem:

> Billie was a pretty hot-tempered woman.... I could see trouble brewing when we went below the Mason-Dixon line and we took her down there, I don't want to repeat the language, but it was rough stuff."[12]

Throughout the tour, Holiday suffered indignity after indignity. She was often refused service at restaurants and diners or was forced to eat in the kitchen, surrounded by her bandmates. In a Kentucky restaurant when another customer uttered a racial slur, Holiday attacked the customer;

she was smuggled out to keep her safe. Because she was the only African American, the discrimination cut even more deeply.

Not only did Shaw have to deal with racism, but he also had other problems to address. Many of those who came to hear Shaw's band were not all that keen on Holiday. Audiences were used to hearing their favorite swing tunes sung in a familiar fashion. Holiday's interpretations of the material were misunderstood. Objections to Holiday's singing were passed on to the ballroom management, which, in turn, complained to Shaw's managers. Now Shaw found himself squeezed; with this ammunition, his managers effectively stopped him from asking for higher booking fees. Shaw scrambled to find a way to solve the problem, and, in the end, hired an additional singer, 19-year-old Helen Forest. In an arrangement similar to that with Nita Bradley, who had since left the band, Forest, who was white, sang the popular numbers while Holiday handled her own material.

By now, Shaw was becoming a hot commodity, with some of the major song publishers after him; many promised to give him exclusive use of their new material. There was only one catch: Holiday was not to sing it. Shaw was caught in a dilemma, but he hoped that the situation would improve as he began to gain more control over his band, its material, and the music publishers. Still, despite Shaw's growing popularity, the band was struggling; as Forest started to get more numbers, Holiday found herself with less and less to do. At one point, Shaw and the band all chipped in to pay Holiday her salary. It is not clear that Holiday was aware of the gesture, but if she was, she must have struggled with feelings of both appreciation and rage.

THE LINCOLN HOTEL

Shaw's big break came when he was booked to play at Manhattan's upscale Lincoln Hotel. The booking was an important one, not only in itself but also because it was broadcast live nationwide over the RCA network. Again, there was a catch; Shaw had the booking, but he had to guarantee the sponsors that Holiday's role would be minimal. During an hour show, she could sing only one or two numbers. The rest of the time she would have to stay in her dressing room. Holiday was not only hurt at the news but also angry.

The worst was to follow. The owner of the hotel took an instant dislike to Holiday, forbidding her to sit at the bar or fraternize with customers. To add to Holiday's anger and humiliation, the owner told Holiday she was to use the tradesmen's entrance and the freight elevator. When Shaw and the other band members learned of these demands, they were outraged. Shaw argued with the owner, but in the end, capitulated. To keep the engagement and allow Holiday to perform at all, Shaw had to see to it that she followed the hotel's rules.

After behaving herself so that Shaw could complete the Lincoln Hotel performance, Holiday could stand it no longer. Less than two weeks into the engagement, she exploded in a rage and quit. She then went to the press, denouncing Shaw and his treatment of her. Shaw angrily refuted her charges, stating that Holiday was up to her old tricks, causing trouble and being unreliable. The friendship ended.

Holiday never modified or retracted her complaints about Shaw, but she also acknowledged Shaw's genius as a musician, along with his help and encouragement. Although disappointed and angry, Shaw bore Holiday no lasting ill will. He was among the first to offer his help when Holiday prepared for her 1953 television comeback show. They remained friendly until her death.

Holiday's collaboration with Shaw turned into another heartbreak for her. Shaw took a courageous stand in her defense, but because of the pressures put on him and his own career demands, he appeared to Holiday to have betrayed and abandoned her. To her credit, Holiday tried to rise above her dubious reputation and a world that could not accept her or understand her talent. In the end, she suffered from racism, and her reputation was worse than before. The tragedy of their situation was that both Shaw and Holiday understood each other's attitudes and actions but were powerless to change society.

Holiday's decision to walk out on Shaw's band did not have entirely negative consequences. Not long afterward, the unlikely duo of a Jewish shoe manufacturer from Trenton, New Jersey, and her friend John Hammond approached her with a proposition. The end result was that Holiday, through the powerful and poignant force of music, at last reached a larger public.

NOTES

1. Billie Holiday, with William Dufty, *Lady Sings the Blues* (New York: Doubleday, 1956), p. 68.

2. Ibid., p. 66.

3. Donald Clarke, *Wishing on the Moon: The Life and Times of Billie Holiday* (New York: Viking, 1994), p. 130.

4. Ibid., p. 132.

5. Ibid.

6. Ibid.

7. Stuart Nicholson, *Billie Holiday* (Boston: Northeastern University Press, 1995), p. 98.

8. Artie Shaw, "Journey of Self Discovery," Dave Radlauer JAZZ Rhythm, http://www.jazzhot.bigstep.com/generic15.html.

9. Ibid.

10. Renee Montague, "Artie Shaw: The Reluctant 'King of Swing' Looks Back on Life on the Throne," NPR, March 8, 2002, http://www.npr.org/programs/morning/features/2002/mar/shaw/.

11. Stuart Nicholson, *Billie Holiday* (Boston: Northeastern University Press, 1995), p. 100.

12. Fred Hall, *Dialogues in Swing* (Ventura, CA: Pathfinder, 1989), p. 134.

In the early 1930s, Elea-
nora Fagan renames herself
Billie Holiday and begins her
singing career by working
in small clubs in New York.
Courtesy of Photofest.

Holiday's career thrives. In
the early 1940s, she performs
at Café Society, the Apollo,
and the Famous Door on 52nd
Street. Courtesy of Photofest.

Billie appears here with a white gardenia in her hair. This flower became a signature trademark that she wore during all her live appearances. Courtesy of Photofest.

Billie in bed. In the mid-1940s, Holiday's personal life begins to decline, causing her to cancel performances. She abuses drugs and alcohol and also suffers from the death of her mother during this time. Courtesy of Photofest.

Billie appears in the role of
Endie, a maid, in the 1947
film New Orleans. Copyright
United Artists. Courtesy of
Photofest.

Holiday at court. Billie finds herself in trouble with the law repeatedly, including an
arrest and incarceration for drug possession in the late 1940s. Courtesy of Photofest.

Billie Holiday joins trumpeter Louis Armstrong for "My Sweet Hunk of Trash," 1949. Courtesy of Photofest.

In the 1950s, Holiday's life is in tatters. She continues to struggle with substance abuse and is involved in a number of abusive relationships. Her performances are periodic and vocally inconsistent. Billie's only attachment appears to be to her beloved Chihuahua, which accompanies her everywhere. Courtesy of Photofest.

Chapter 6

"STRANGE FRUIT"

By the end of 1938, Billie Holiday's spirits were low; she no longer had a job and had few prospects in sight. To make matters worse, she was frustrated about her inability to reach a larger audience. At the same time, her relations with Hammond were becoming more strained.

The crisis with Hammond had come a few months earlier, at a November recording session. Holiday was unhappy with arrangements that she found too lyric-heavy, giving her little room to bring her signature style to the songs. The session was mediocre at best, leaving Holiday angry and Hammond frustrated. When Hammond decided to exclude Holiday from his upcoming concert *From Spirituals to Swing*, slated to open on December 23, 1938, at Carnegie Hall, she went into a rage. After another recording session on January 30, 1939, Holiday and Hammond parted ways. Despite their growing animosity, Holiday and Hammond managed a last successful collaboration. Backed by Teddy Wilson, Benny Carter, and Roy Eldridge, Holiday added another classic to her repertoire with her rendition of "More Than You Know."

Even more ironic, Hammond's last booking for Billie proved to be the one that at last introduced her to a mass audience. What's more, a tune that Billie introduced that night sent shock waves through the jazz world and became one of the most powerful and haunting songs of the twentieth century.

CAFÉ SOCIETY

In the closing years of the Depression, Barney Josephson, an intrepid New Jersey shoe salesman, had a dream. He wanted to open a supper club. Born in Trenton, New Jersey, Josephson wanted to do more with his life than sell shoes. He moved to New York City where he lived with his brother's family.

Possessed of a sharp intellect and with a left-wing political consciousness, Josephson decided his club would be a place to mock the so-called Smart Set, his potential clientele. He drew on a popular trend that began to emerge during the late 1930s. Some nightspots, such as El Dumpo in Chicago, deliberately made fun of their customers. Waiters were intentionally rude to them, spilled soup in their laps, and so forth. Josephson, however, wanted greater subtly in his approach. More than making fun of his potential clientele, Josephson wanted his club to feature jazz and to be racially integrated.

The problem was that Josephson did not know much about jazz or even how to book the best talent. His quest led him to John Hammond; the two men quickly took a liking to each other and soon Hammond agreed to book musicians for Café Society, as Josephson's club was called. In the meantime, Josephson set about preparing for opening night. Ivan Black, whom Jospehson had hired to do publicity, worked overtime to make sure that people knew about the newest hotspot, promising that Café Society would present jazz "for the first time with dignity and respect."[1]

Housed in an old speakeasy located in Sheridan Square on West 4th Street, Café Society opened its doors on December 30, 1938. For opening night, Hammond had lined up trumpeter Frankie Newton and his band, with Billie Holiday as the featured attraction. Everything finally appeared to be ready. With doormen wearing raggedy suits and white gloves, Café Society was advertised as "a nightclub to take the stuffing out of stuffed shirts" and "the wrong place for the Right people."[2] It was unlike anything New York society had ever seen. The club mocked the celebrity worship, right-wing politics, and racial segregation of other nightspots, such as the exclusive Stork Club. Opening night was not perfect. Josephson had trouble getting liquor and cabaret licenses, the latter permitting live entertainment. Because the kitchen was not yet open, hot dogs were delivered from the hot-dog stand across the street and the liquor license finally arrived at 11:30 P.M., and not a moment too soon.

By that hour, the club was packed with more than 600 persons, even though the fire code set the legal limit at 210. Josephson's hunch had paid off; the people loved everything about the club, from its murals to the table cards and programs that continued the theme of ribbing Café Society. Jack Gilford, a comedian who opened the show, made fun of snobbery as part of his act, to the delight of the audience. Billie Holiday also enjoyed a warm reception from the crowd, later earning rave reviews from local music critics. All in all, the evening was a resounding success. Everyone from movie stars to writers, critics, and jazz aficionados found something to like at New York's hottest new club.

For Billie, Hammond's final booking was the boost her career needed. Not only did her time at Café Society allow her to develop her style, it also afforded her the exposure she desperately sought. Even though she had sung with both Artie Shaw's and Count Basie's orchestras and had a number of recordings to her credit, Holiday still was not well known outside of Harlem. Café Society changed all that, as Holiday became one the top draws for the club. This popularity finally gave Holiday more control over her material. She could now pick her own songs and approve their arrangements.

With this new power, and the freedom that went with it, Holiday's singing became even more sophisticated and nuanced than before. The stint at Café Society allowed her to reach deeper within herself and fill out the persona she had been creating over the years: the woman unlucky in love, destined never to pick the right man or to be happy, and to sing about her misery.

MR. MEEROPOL

Abel Meeropol is best remembered as the man who stepped forward to raise the two sons of executed spies Julius and Ethel Rosenberg. Meeropol made his living as an English teacher in the Bronx, a position that he held for 27 years. In addition to his teaching duties, Meeropol was a political activist. Both he and his wife belonged to the Communist Party, to which he donated a portion of his earnings. Meeropol was also a poet and songwriter.

Often writing under the name "Lewis Allan," Meeropol wrote a variety of poems, ballads, and musicals. Many of his songs were of a topical nature, such as "A Red under My Bed," a reference to anti-Communist fears that many Americans harbored during the 1950s, and "The Chamberlain Crawl," a song about British Prime Minister Neville Chamberlain's efforts to appease Adolph Hitler before World War II. Meeropol counted among his fans noted lyricist Ira Gershwin and the German composer Kurt Weill.

Sometime in 1930, Meeropol was reading a civil rights magazine that had published a particularly gruesome photo of a double lynching of two black men in Indiana. Sickened and haunted by the image, Meeropol also realized that the incident was far from isolated.

Lynchings, indeed, were nothing new in America; they were rooted in the American tradition of vigilantism, or taking the law into one's own hands, to punish criminals and outlaws. The word *lynching* originated in Bedford County, Virginia, during the Revolutionary War when Colonel Charles Lynch and other patriots organized to catch and punish Tories as well as other criminals. Lynch's actions led to the term *lynch law,* in which undesirables were punished by whippings, tarring and feathering, and occasionally hangings or shootings. At first, the victims of lynching were mostly white, and ranged from petty criminals to Catholics and immigrants. By the 1830s, however, lynching had taken on overtly racial overtones. Blacks were now the chief victims.

THE SHAME OF AMERICA

At its height, between 1882 and 1956, lynching in the United States caused the deaths of more than 4,700 men, women, and children; of that number, more than 80 percent were black. By the beginning of the twentieth century, lynching, with few exceptions, was confined to the South. Public hangings still took place, but by this time lynching had devolved into a horrific spectacle of torture that often involved mutilation and burning of the body. Many journalists publicized these enormities in an effort to get a federal law passed to ban the practice. A black schoolteacher turned journalist, Ida B. Wells-Barnett, continued to report lynchings in her newspaper, the *Memphis Free Speech and Headlight,* even under threats of violence. The *Chicago Tribune* began to run an annual tally of lynchings in 1882. In 1912, the *Crisis,* the official publication of the National Association for the Advancement of Colored People (NAACP), compiled a similar list under the headline "The Shame of America."

In 1919, a year of deadly race riots in the United States, the House of Representatives debated an antilynching bill. By a vote of 230 to 119, the House approved the Dyer Anti-Lynching Bill in 1922. Introduced by Representative L. C. Dyer of Missouri, the bill asserted the duty of the federal government to protect the civil rights of individuals, echoing the Fifteenth Amendment and anticipating the Civil Rights Act of 1964. Southerners such as John Sharp Williams and Pat Harrison of Mississippi, who dominated the Senate, prevented the Dyer Bill from coming to a vote. Yet, members of Congress persisted in trying to enact an antilynching measure throughout the 1930s and 1940s. Southern legislators, however, were powerful and influential. They managed to kill every bill that came to the floor for a vote. Despite the failure of Congress to outlaw lynching, the number of lynchings in the South declined after 1935, but did not cease altogether until 1981.

STRANGE FRUIT

For Abel Meeropol and others like him, the shocking images of lynching published in the newspapers and magazines cut to the heart. Meeropol could not get the image out of his mind. He finally wrote a poem about lynching entitled "Bitter Fruit," which appeared in the January 1937 issue of the *New York Teacher*, a union publication. Meeropol then set the poem to music; by the late 1930s, the song was regularly performed in the left-wing circles Meeropol frequented, including a version by a black singer named Laura Duncan. After hearing Duncan sing Meeropol's song at an anti-Fascist fundraiser, promoter Robert Gordon, who was putting together the first floor show at Café Society, thought it would be a good vehicle for Billie Holiday. Barney Josephson recalled that "one of the first numbers we put on was called: '*Strange Fruit Grows on Southern Trees*' the tragic story of lynching. Imagine putting that on in a night club!"[3]

How the song became one of Billie Holiday's signature numbers is, like so many aspects of her life, fraught with ambiguity and contradiction. Early in 1939, at Jospehson's and Gordon's invitation, Meeropol visited Café Society. (Josephson later stated that Meeropol unexpectedly showed up at the club.) No matter the circumstances, Meeropol presented Josephson with a song entitled "Strange Fruit." Josephson admitted that "he was floored" by the lyrics, but was unsure what to do with the song.[4] Meeropol asked whether Billie Holiday would consider singing it. He played the song for Billie, who seemed to Meeropol unimpressed. "To be perfectly frank, I didn't think she felt very comfortable with the song, because it was so different from the songs to which she was accustomed," Meeropol later wrote.[5]

Josephson thought that Holiday did not understand the meaning of the song and only agreed to sing it as a favor to him. Not until several months later, when he spotted a tear running down her cheek during a performance, did he feel the meaning of the song had sunk in. "But I gotta tell you the truth," Josephson later said, "she sang it just as well when she didn't know what it was about."[6]

The assumption that Billie did not understand the meaning of "Strange Fruit" is dubious. She may have been without formal education, but she was not stupid. Meeropol said later that when Holiday sang the song "she gave a startling, most dramatic, and effective interpretation ... which could jolt an audience out of its complacency anywhere.... Billie Holiday's styling of the song was incomparable and fulfilled the bitterness and shocking quality I had hoped the song would have."[7]

For Holiday, "Strange Fruit" required more of her than any song she had ever performed. As biographer Stuart Nicholson noted, "'Strange

Fruit' was not an 'I' (Billie) talking to 'you' (the listeners) as was the case with many of her songs. 'Strange Fruit' required of Billie a whole new level of interpretation, one that asked her to interpret a terrible social condition for the audience."[8]

"Strange Fruit" is filled with strong imagery and emotion; Meeropol described lynching in a manner that almost seems incongruent with the subject. The "strange fruit" referred to in the song are the bodies of African American men hanged during a lynching. The song was clearly not typical of the music for which Holiday had become known. Her genius lay in the ability to transform even the most banal lyric and simple melody into something emotionally vivid and poignant. "Strange Fruit" had a raw power of its own that forced Holiday to confront some of the most painful aspects of her life. At 24, she, like most blacks, knew intimately the sting of racism. "Strange Fruit" offered a chilling and unsettling reminder of her place in the world.

Of the first time she performed "Strange Fruit," Holiday said: "The first time I sang it, I thought it was a mistake. There wasn't even a patter of applause when I finished. Then a lone person began to clap nervously. Then suddenly everyone was clapping."[9] Stuart Nicholson wrote that the song forced the white, middle-class audience to confront the reality of racism and lynching. Never before had a song so directly dealt with such a controversial issue.[10]

Josephson's theatrics added to the drama and emotion of Holiday's performance. First, he told Holiday to close each of her three nightly sets with "Strange Fruit." Second, before she sang, all service in the club was halted. Third, the room was to be completely dark, except for the spotlight that illuminated Holiday's face. No matter how much the audience applauded, Holiday was never to return to the stage once she had left it. "My instruction was walk on, period," Josephson later said. "People had to remember 'Strange Fruit,' get their insides burned with it."[11]

MIXED REACTIONS

Not everyone knew what to make of Holiday's new material. *Variety*, a newspaper devoted to show business news, called "Strange Fruit" "basically a depressing piece."[12] At Café Society, some patrons, offended by the song, walked out. One distraught woman confronted Holiday in a powder room at the club, screeching at her never to sing the song again. It turned out that the woman had seen a black man tied up and dragged behind a car through the streets of her town, hanged, and then burned. As Josephson stated, the patron had come for an evening of entertainment, not to relive a horrible childhood experience.[13] Even Holiday's mother hated the song, asking her daughter why she was risking her career and possibly even her life to sing "Strange Fruit":

> "Why are you sticking your neck out?" she [Sadie] asked.
> "Because it might make things better," Holiday replied.
> "But you'd be dead," her mother insisted.
> "Yeah, but I'll feel it. I'll know it in my grave."[14]

"Strange Fruit" had more than its share of supporters, too. People began requesting the song, and it soon became part of Holiday's regular set, even though singing it made her sick. "I have to sing it," she once said. "'Fruit' goes a long way in telling how they mistreat Negroes down South."[15] As news of the song spread, Josephson began advertising not just Billie Holiday as Café Society's featured performer, but he also publicized the song in the hope of drawing even more patrons to the club.

AN UNFORGETTABLE SONG

Judging by public reaction, Billie had struck a chord with "Strange Fruit"; soon talks began about the possibility of recording it. When Columbia Records was approached, however, record executives declined, fearful of antagonizing Southern customers. Surprised, hurt, and angry, Billie turned to Milt Gabler, the founder of Commodore Records, a small company run out of a music store on West 52nd Street. In an interview given years later, Gabler remembered:

> Billie was very sad, she had this great number that was so important to her and they wouldn't let her record it. I told her if she could get a one-session release from her contract I'd like to have her do it for Commodore.[16]

On April 20, 1939, at the Brunswick's World Broadcasting Studios, Billie Holiday met with Frankie Newton's Café Society Band, including Sonny White on piano, Frankie Newton on trumpet, Tab Smith on alto sax, Kenneth Holton and Stan Payne on tenor sax, Jimmy McLin on guitar, John Williams on bass, and Eddie Dougherty on drums. The outcome of the session was the recording of the first and probably the most famous rendition of "Strange Fruit." Gabler paid Holiday five hundred dollars for "Strange Fruit" and three other songs that she recorded that day; she later received a second payment of one thousand dollars. How much Holiday earned from her recording is uncertain, as Gabler paid her in cash right out of the store's register. Abel Meeropol, who had failed to copyright the song, learned of the recording when a friend brought him a copy. After negotiating with Commodore, he earned royalties, which, over time, amounted to more than three hundred thousand dollars.

Released on July 22, 1939, "Strange Fruit" rose to number 16 on the record charts, selling 10,000 copies in its first week. Despite, or perhaps because of, the controversy surrounding the song, people bought the recording as soon as it appeared in shops. Stories circulated that radio stations in both America and Great Britain were refusing to play it.

Reviews of the recording were mixed. *Time* reprinted the first verse of the song, describing it as "a prime piece of musical propaganda" for the NAACP. The reviewer could not resist taking a few gratuitous jabs at Holiday: "Billie Holiday is a roly-poly young colored woman with a hump in her voice. She does not care enough about her figure to watch her diet, but she loves to sing."[17] Writing for the *New York Post*, Samuel Grafton was more positive. "'Strange Fruit' ... makes you blink and hold to your chair. Even now, as I think of it, the short hair on the back of my neck tightens and I want to hit somebody. I know who, too."[18] The song also garnered political attention when advocates of federal antilynching legislation urged that copies be sent to members of Congress.

Holiday's reaction to the song, like that of many of her critics, was mixed. "Strange Fruit" has "a way of separating the straight people from the squares and cripples," she wrote in her autobiography. She recalled the time that a woman in Los Angeles asked her to sing "that sexy song" she was so famous for—"you know, the one about the naked bodies swinging in the trees." Holiday refused. At a club outside Los Angeles, a young white man shouted racist remarks at Holiday; she later noted that, "After two shows of this I was ready to quit.... I knew if I didn't the third time round I might bounce something off that cracker and land in some ... jail." As it turned out, Holiday did not have to take matters into her own hands. Instead, Bob Hope, who was at the club with Judy Garland, badgered the heckler until he left.

LEGACY

For Billie Holiday, the decision to perform and record "Strange Fruit" was a watershed in her career. As a result, she enjoyed an acclaim that had eluded her for years. She was even gaining recognition beyond the music world. Yet, for jazz purists, "Strange Fruit" had strangled Holiday's talent. Writing in *Down Beat*, a poplar music magazine, one critic declared: "Perhaps I expected too much of 'Strange Fruit,' the ballyhooed

... tune which, via gory wordage and hardly any melody, expounds an anti-lynching campaign.... At least I'm sure it's not for Billie."[19] Perhaps even more hurtful to Holiday were the comments of her mentor John Hammond. He called it "the beginning of the end for Billie" and "artistically the worst thing that ever happened to her." For him, Holiday had simply become too serious. "The more conscious she was of her style, the more mannered she became," he later said.[20] By taking herself so seriously, she had lost her artistry and her sparkle.

After performing at Café Society for almost two years, Holiday left in 1940. Although she found work in other clubs, many owners refused to let her sing "Strange Fruit," which eventually prompted Holiday to demand a clause in her contracts specifying that she could perform the song whenever she wanted. Holiday performed the song at the Apollo Theater several times. Jack Schifrman, whose family ran the Apollo, recalled that initially his father did not want Holiday to sing "Strange Fruit," fearing trouble from audiences. But according to his son, his fears were put to rest the first time Holiday performed "Strange Fruit":

> When she wrenched the final words from her lips, there was not a soul in that audience, black or white, who did not feel half strangled.... A moment of oppressively heavy silence followed, and then a kind of rustling sound I had never heard before. It was the sound of almost two thousand people sighing.[21]

"Strange Fruit" remained a fixture in Holiday's shows until she died. The song never lost its power for Holiday, and she never lost her passion for the song; it seemed as though her anger and sorrow at the racial indignities she had suffered filled her performances with an intensity that few other singers could muster. Club managers continued to find ways to underscore the song's inherent drama; one maitre d' at New York's Birdland actually confiscated all cigarettes, so that she could perform in darkness with only a small pinpoint of light on her face. Even after Holiday's battle with drugs and alcohol had left her dissipated, she could still draw from a deep and powerful force within her that always left people moved.

"Strange Fruit" continues to belong to Billie Holiday. In the years since her death, other performers have recorded it, but the song remains Billie's. It is as personal to her as her fingerprints or her signature. It is her riveting interpretation that listeners remember. It is her voice that calls the song to life—her voice that conveys its pain and its sorrow. "Frankly, I don't think anybody but Billie should do it," stated Dan Morgenstern, director of the Institute of Jazz Studies at Rutgers in a recent interview. "I don't think anybody can improve on it."[22] In 1999, *Time*, perhaps offering a belated amends to Holiday, named "Strange Fruit" the "Best Song of the Twentieth Century."

NOTES

1. Stuart Nicholson, *Billie Holiday* (Boston: Northeastern University Press, 1995), p. 111.

2. David Margolick, "Strange Fruit," *Vanity Fair*, September 1998, http://www.vanityfair.com/commentary/content/articles/050912roco01a.

3. Ibid.

4. David Margolick, *Strange Fruit: Billie Holiday, Café Society and the Early Cry for Civil Rights* (Philadelphia: Running Press, 2000), p. 42.

5. Ibid., p. 43.

6. Ibid.

7. Ibid., p. 46.

8. Quoted in Ibid.

9. Billie Holiday, with William Dufty, *Lady Sings the Blues* (New York: Doubleday, 1956), p. 83.

10. Nicholson, *Billie Holiday*, p. 111.

11. Margolick, *Strange Fruit*, p. 45.

12. Ibid., p. 63.

13. Margolick "Strange Fruit."

14. Ibid., p. 65.

15. Holiday, *Lady Sings the Blues*, p. 84.

16. Nicholson, *Billie Holiday*, p. 113.

17. "Strange Record," *Time*, June 12, 1939, http://www.time.com/time/archive/preview/0,10987,762422,00.html.

18. Margolick, "Strange Fruit."

19. Ibid.

20. Nicholson, *Billie Holiday*, pp. 113–14.

21. Donald Clarke, *Wishing on the Moon: The Life and Times of Billie Holiday* (New York: Viking, 1994), p. 115.

22. Margolick, "Strange Fruit."

Chapter 7

LIFE AS BILLIE HOLIDAY

With the boost from "Strange Fruit," Billie Holiday entered one of her most prolific periods. Not only did she hit the peak of her popularity, but her records sold well, and she was commanding salaries she had once only dreamt about. But Holiday paid a price for her growing success; her relationship with Hammond was strained, her friendship with Artie Shaw was broken, she was drinking more, and her drug use had increased. In addition to these problems was her inability to sustain relationships with men. Like her mother, Holiday was drawn to men who treated her badly. Sometimes she ended love affairs quickly or entertained herself with one-night stands. Although Holiday took these experiences and melded them into her stage persona, in real life, she was often lonely and depressed.

The impact of "Strange Fruit" also changed the way Holiday conducted herself in the recording studio. She became more discerning about her material and more conscious of how she sang and interacted with a group of musicians. By 1940, Holiday could no longer be called simply a female vocalist. Instead, she began favoring carefully arranged material that kept the focus on her, allowing only arranged solo interludes by another musician. Missing from both her recordings and her live performances were the more spontaneous improvisations that she had experimented with early in her career. She was now a vocal actress, who translated words and music into something filled with dramatic tension, heartbreak, and sadness or interpreted something happy, vital, and free.

MOVING ON

While still employed at Café Society, Holiday played other venues. By the end of 1939, she had performed at the Hippodrome in New York City, the Apollo, and the Uptown House. She also found time to get in the recording studio where she recorded a number of songs that became Holiday favorites, including "Them There Eyes," "Some Other Spring," and "Long Gone Blues." Many musicians found her to be in top form, professional, and easy to work with. Many also commented on Holiday's maverick nature and the fact that she did what she liked, regardless of the consequences. If she wanted to drink or take drugs, she did. Her bisexuality led to dates and affairs with both men and women. As Josephson recalled, Holiday never apologized, for she was not ashamed of her life. She wanted to have fun in whatever way she could. Still, Josephson realized that her behavior was also tragic and destructive. Her habits would ultimately create more demons for her to battle.

Even as Billie Holiday was making a name for herself at Café Society, the winds of change were in the air. She found herself competing with the boogie-woogie pianists who were becoming popular at the beginning of the 1940s. Boogie-woogie was a style of blues piano playing that soon incorporated other instruments and eventually was popularized by the big bands. The style originated from the dance music known as barrelhouse blues that was popular among poorer African Americans in the South. The musical form really began to take shape when the music developed a faster, purely instrumental form of blues for dancing. The boogie-woogie musicians soon became the top draw at Café Society while Holiday became known as the "queen of song."[1]

Holiday's final performance at Café Society was in early November 1939. Two weeks later, she was gone and a new singer was in her place. Holiday wanted more money. Her demands arose not from wanting to leave the club but from wanting to stay. She had earlier received an offer from another club owner at Ernie's in the Village, who would hire her for more money than she was earning at Café Society. Holiday simply wanted Josephson to pay her the same amount. When he refused, she had no choice but to leave. It marked the end of a remarkable partnership for both. Still Holiday's move to Ernie's paid off: she played to standing-room only audiences every night. However, she never forgot what Josephson had done for her and would later say, "I opened Café Society as an unknown, I left two years later as a star."[2]

THE STREET

For the next several months, Holiday was booked in the clubs that lined the area of 52nd Street between Fifth and Sixth avenues, known as "the

Street." Many of the clubs and restaurants were similar to those found in Harlem; several had started as speakeasies during Prohibition and often were little more than small rooms with a kitchen, a tiny bandstand, a bar, and tables and chairs. As one jazz writer commented, the clubs were dark, smoky, and served terrible liquor, but they were the perfect place to listen to jazz.

Initially, many of the hotspots were strictly segregated, meaning that the only African Americans allowed into these establishments were those who worked or performed there. The segregation policy was so restrictive that, at one point, Holiday likened working the Street to working as a slave on a plantation. Slowly, however, the climate was changing. With the opening of Café Society and the first integrated jazz group headed by Benny Goodman playing at various spots, some of the clubs relented and eventually relaxed the rules of "white only." Soon, the whole street took on the air of a giant house party, with each club featuring some of the best acts in jazz. Because the clubs were so close together, it was common to catch one musician playing with one group early in the evening and then later to spot him at a club down the street playing with an entirely new group. The combination led to an important contribution to jazz history; out of these jazz sessions came more improvised sessions that were held after hours that gave birth to another classic jazz form known as "bebop." By the end of the 1940s, this new sound completely overtook the big bands.

By this time, Holiday was the neighborhood's biggest headliner, drawing huge crowds wherever she sang. She earned close to one thousand dollars a week (approximately fourteen thousand in today's dollars) and was, by all accounts, one of the most successful African American jazz performers in the United States and abroad. Her popularity was so great that many clubs did away with advertising and instead counted on word of mouth to draw audiences in. People came not only to hear her sing, but to watch her entrance, which usually entailed walking in slowly with one or two dogs in tow. She moved majestically to the stage and, once settled, began her performance. Holiday was regal in her performances, holding her head high while she told her stories, singing right to the heart of every song she performed.

At her peak vocally, Billie Holiday was also at her most beautiful physically. A large woman, she now could afford beautiful evening gowns and jewelry that emphasized and flattered her figure; she even offered tips on make-up and dress for magazine articles aimed at African American women. During the early 1940s she also adopted what would become her

signature trademark: a white gardenia worn in her hair. While performing at Kelly's Stable, Holiday singed her hair with a curling iron. Another jazz singer appearing at the club went to another club where the
hat-check girls were selling flowers and bought a large white gardenia for
Holiday to pin over the burned section of her hair. Holiday liked the look
so much that the white gardenia became a staple in every live appearance
she made. Even after her death, the white gardenia has become as much a
part of Holiday's iconography as her name Lady Day.

A BUSY LIFE

In early January 1940, Holiday met a man at a friend's birthday party.
His name was James Monroe, the brother of Clark Monroe, the owner
of the Uptown House where Holiday often sang. James was known as a
sportsman, a term used for those who were involved in unsavory activities such as prostitution and selling drugs. Monroe was handsome and a
bit of a dandy, wearing the latest fashions, and he possessed a street attitude to which Holiday was immediately drawn. He had recently returned
from Europe, where he ran a Paris nightclub. But with the storm clouds of
war rapidly approaching, Monroe left and returned to New York. While
Billie saw a man confident and unconcerned about impressing people, her
friends saw something different in James Monroe: a dark and violent man
looking for a meal ticket.

Holiday's attraction to Monroe came shortly after the end of a yearlong
love affair with jazz pianist Sonny White. According to friends, White
was deeply in love with Holiday and she with him. The affair was intense
and emotional. As both still lived with their mothers, however, any marriage plans they might have entertained fell apart. Years of living with
Sadie, listening to the constant tirades against men and her father's un-
faithfulness, compounded her daughter's inabilities to sustain a healthy
relationship. She turned to men like Monroe, who abused and exploited
her. Monroe was no different. Within days of their meeting, he hit Holiday in public in front of a club. Holiday told Sadie she had been mugged.

Not long after meeting Monroe, Holiday was back in the studio in
February 1940 to begin recording another record for Columbia. The session overall was dark and moody, in part because of Holiday's choice of
material, which included the song "Ghost of Yesterday." Holiday also
recorded the standard "Body and Soul," which also became part of her
songbook. No sooner had she finished than she was off to a series of dates
that took her through New York City and Chicago. While in Chicago,

she made nightly radio broadcasts live from the exclusive Hotel Sherman. Then it was back to New York City. In early May, she was asked to appear on another popular New York radio program, but upon hearing that Ella Fitzgerald would be there, she did not show up on broadcast day. She did, though, show up to do a spot on another local radio show where she drew rave reviews for her performance.

In August 1940, she agreed to do another song by Lewis Allan (Abel Meeropal), who wrote "Strange Fruit." Titled "Over Here: The Yanks Aren't Coming," the song was a parody of Irving Berlin's popular hit, "Over There: The Yanks Are Coming," which he wrote for the American troops during World War I. Like "Strange Fruit," "Over Here" was a protest song, condemning the lack of American involvement in Europe's war with Hitler. The United States would not enter the war until late 1941 when the Japanese bombed the U.S. naval base at Pearl Harbor, Hawaii. Allan's song enjoyed a modest success but not everyone found it funny or was taken with Holiday's singing. In the fall of 1940, the FBI approached Ralph Watkins, owner of Kelly's Stables, where Holiday was performing at the time. The agents told Watkins to stop Holiday from singing the song, which was considered by some government officials to be unpatriotic. When Watkins told Holiday, she was outraged; in the end, though, there was little she could do except accede to Watkins's request. But the matter did not end there; because of Holiday's perceived left-wing tendencies, the FBI started a file: "#4855389-Billie Holiday: Singer."[3]

THE NEW MAN

In the meantime, Holiday kept busy with singing engagements through the end of 1940 and well into 1941. In October 1940, she agreed to come back to the original Café Society, and, in addition, open Josephson's latest venture, Café Society uptown. Holiday was still performing at the Apollo Theater; on opening night, she raced from downtown to uptown, making her performances on time. Josephson, though, was unhappy with the arrangement; he did not want Holiday having two bookings. However, the two arranged a compromise that allowed her to finish her contract with the Apollo while singing at Café Society uptown. In December, just after the holidays, Holiday left Café Society to begin a new job at Kelly's Stables, where she had performed off and on into the middle of 1941. Holiday's first open-air concert was on May 1, 1941, where she performed "Strange Fruit." Then it was back to Kelly's Stables where she continued to perform until June.

Holiday's next booking was not until mid-July. Until then, she spent her time with James Monroe visiting the Uptown House. While there, she regularly sat in with the house band. In the meantime, Monroe was becoming a bigger part of her life: seeing himself as a self-styled impresario, he told Holiday how to conduct herself now that she was a star. He even took over the more mundane details of her life, such as selecting her wardrobe. By now, Holiday's popularity was such that she was making a great deal of money, only to spend it on a growing band of hangers-on who were only interested in a free handout. She and Sadie fought often over Monroe, whom Sadie forbade to come to the house. Holiday became even more defiant, and, despite her mother's pleas, continued to see Monroe. Sadie had other reasons to dislike Monroe: since he settled into her daughter's life, Sadie was not getting the attention or the money she once was from Holiday. In spite of Holiday's setting her mother up in a business venture, a restaurant located on 99th and Amsterdam, Sadie's complaints were ongoing. Holiday's agent, Joe Glaser, also voiced his disapproval of Holiday's latest beau.

MARRIED LIFE

On August 23, 1941, at 10:55 P.M., the Reverend William F. Hopkins of Elkton, Maryland, was awakened. There was a couple waiting to be married. After applying for a marriage license, Hopkins performed the ceremony, uniting in marriage Billie Holiday and James Monroe. The two had come to Washington, D.C., a week earlier to begin Holiday's newest singing job at the Howard Theater. Besides celebrating her marriage, Holiday could celebrate something else too: Columbia Records rereleased an album of eight songs that Holiday had recorded with Teddy Wilson, dating back to their first recording session in 1935. Reviews of the record were positive, and, in many cases, enthusiastic, as critics lauded the work as a true jazz gem.

Upon her return from Washington, Holiday got ready to leave for Chicago to appear again at the Sherman Hotel with bandleader Lionel Hampton. But first she had to face Sadie to break the news of her marriage. Sadie was angry and sad. A friend of the family who was visiting Sadie witnessed the meeting and remembered that, as the two were arguing, Holiday became so angry, she threw down her marriage license and asked sarcastically of Sadie that since she and Monroe were married, could he now come into the house.[4] Depressed at the turn of events, Sadie could do nothing and would chalk her inability to stop Holiday as another instance of her poor parenting, particularly her inability to keep her daughter from making such poor choices when it came to men.

After her time in Chicago, Holiday was off again—this time to Los Angeles, where she was to perform at a club also known as Café Society. Opening in October, Holiday performed at the club nightly, backed by a band of local musicians. She quickly became a favorite of many Hollywood celebrities, who came to see her night after night. But her popularity did little to help the club; after only three weeks, Café Society unexpectedly shut down, leaving Holiday with no paycheck and hardly enough money to make it back to New York. In the meantime, Monroe told Holiday that he was going to stay on the West Coast for a little while longer; it turned out that Monroe, who had a reputation as a drug dealer, had made connections with a drug ring to bring in marijuana from across the Mexican border. Holiday went back east alone.

She had little time to think about her marriage. Upon her arrival in New York, she was immediately booked to play at the Apollo and then at the Famous Door on 52nd Street. Holiday noticed that the musical atmosphere was changing. Younger musicians were now gathering after hours to experiment with new ideas. These musical experiments marked the beginning of a new musical style known as bebop, in which the stylized and more rhythmic flow of a song was replaced by broken phrases. Although Holiday listened to the new sound, she remained indifferent to it, continuing to refine her own style.

The year 1941 saw the release of several songs that, along with "Strange Fruit," came to be associated with Holiday: "Gloomy Sunday" (one of Holiday's personal favorites), "Am I Blue," "Solitude," "I Cover the Waterfront," and "God Bless the Child." The latter was the only song that Holiday co-wrote. Stories differ about how the song came to be, but the main theme was surely of Holiday's own choosing. After lamenting to a songwriter friend how Sadie refused to lend her some money (other stories have Sadie asking for money from Holiday), Holiday exclaimed, "God bless the child." When asked to explain, Holiday replied:

> That's what we used to say—your mother's got money, your father's got money, your sister's got money, your cousin's got money, but if you haven't got it yourself, God bless the child that's got his own.[5]

However the song's lyrics came about, "God Bless the Child" was a hit for Holiday. It was the last hit record she ever had.

For many jazz experts and critics, the above songs were storytelling songs; that is, melodies that are told in a kind of narrative. Although the songs themselves lean toward the sentimental, Holiday's singing of them brought forth deep emotion. Along with her love songs, Holiday's performances no doubt resonated with audiences in wartime when all Americans felt longing, sadness, and loss.

Without any explanation in early January 1942, Holiday left her job at the Famous Door to perform in Montreal. No one is still quite sure why she left; what is known is that she was replaced by another singer. In February 1942, Holiday returned to New York City for what would be her last recording session with Columbia Records. The sessions lacked the vitality and heart of her earlier sessions in 1940 to 1941.

With the war on, people were more concerned with events in Europe and the Pacific. By early 1942, the music industry also was suffering through a yearlong strike, in which the American Federation of Musicians imposed a recording ban, demanding they be paid a fee for every record broadcast on radio. Many musicians and singers lost out on valuable exposure because of the strike. Musical tastes were changing; in September 1942, a new singing sensation, Frank Sinatra, was wowing crowds, and, in the process, ushering in a new era of popular music. As labels began scrambling to sign up new talent, one name was conspicuously absent from contract talks: Billie Holiday, who now was labeled as too difficult to work with.

THE END OF AN ERA

By the time she had stepped out of the Columbia studio in 1942, Holiday had recorded 153 songs for the company, beginning with her first session in 1933 with Benny Goodman. Within that decade, Holiday recorded what many consider to be her finest body of work, showcasing her growth as a singer and performer. In the beginning, her work was free of self-consciousness as she sang honestly about the foibles of love and life. Musically untrained, Holiday had the capacity to learn up to four new songs in a recording session. Sometimes, she was lucky to run through the songs the day before, but more often than not, Holiday was learning them as the session began. Still, the songs emerged as something unique, a visible sign of her sophisticated and innovative musical mind.

Working with some of the best musicians in the business, Holiday used her voice in ways that were new and innovative. In the beginning, her singing was like one of the instruments in the band; as she matured, her voice became vital to creating and shaping the persona she lived and sung about: unlucky in love and aware of life's frailties. In a short period of time, Holiday not only grew as an artist, but she also defined herself. What followed never matched the accomplishments of those earlier years.

NOTES

1. Stuart Nicholson, *Billie Holiday* (Boston: Northeastern University Press, 1995), p. 118.

2. Robert O'Meally, *Lady Day: The Many Faces of Billie Holiday* (New York: Little, Brown, 1991), p. 148.

3. Nicholson, *Billie Holiday*, p. 121.

4. Donald Clarke, *Wishing on the Moon: The Life and Times of Billie Holiday* (New York: Viking, 1994), p. 135.

5. Ibid., p. 123.

Chapter 8

A SLOW DESCENT INTO HELL

When Billie's contract with Columbia Records expired in 1942, she was temporarily without a label, but not without work. Her manager, Joe Glaser, had other plans for her. Glaser's approach was to keep Holiday in the public eye by lining up brief singing dates in different cities rather than putting her on longer tours. This time she traveled with bandleader Benny Carter for a series of theater dates. Glaser's reasoning was simple: short runs made more money than long ones.

When presented with the itinerary, however, Holiday exploded, stating that Glaser might cover the United States with phone calls, but she had to do it the hard way by traveling hundreds of miles. Despite her hard feelings toward Glaser, Holiday did have to admit that he really had her interests at heart, which included Holiday receiving top dollar for her performances. As it was, she was running out of money and battling a reputation that labeled her unreliable and difficult. In April 1942, Holiday set off, first playing the Apollo before moving on to Cleveland, where Holiday and Carter opened at a new nightspot. Business, though, was only middling, and, after only two weeks, the engagement ended when the club closed.

MORE BAD NEWS

Once again, as Holiday was making some strides forward, bad news stepped in the way. Getting ready to leave for Cleveland, Holiday learned that her husband, James Monroe, had been arrested for drug smuggling. With his arraignment scheduled for the end of May, Holiday had less than a month to raise the needed money to help pay for his legal defense. Upon her arrival on the West Coast, Holiday found that her friends Lee and Lester Young were working in Los Angeles. They persuaded their boss at the Trouville Club to hire Holiday as part of the group. The owner agreed. Soon thereafter, Holiday was regularly performing at the club, where she became the darling of the Hollywood set.

When Monroe's case finally came to trial, the jury found him guilty as charged and he was sentenced to a year in jail. Holiday's efforts were wasted; her job at the Trouville paid Monroe's legal expenses but left her almost with nothing. She was also about to be evicted from her apartment along with another musician, Trummy Young, whom Holiday had started seeing. To earn some money, Young gave a song he had written to Johnny Mercer, one of the country's leading songwriters. He, along with two others, had recently established a new record label called Capitol Records. Mercer agreed to take Young's song, and, after adding lyrics, passed the song on for the final arranging. It was decided that the Paul Whiteman Orchestra would record the song; Holiday, under the name "Lady Day," would sing. Both she and Young ended up making seventy-five dollars apiece, enough to pay the hotel bill, eat a Chinese dinner, and go to some clubs. After the celebration was over, Holiday, with five dollars in her pocket, wired her mother for money to pay for both her and Young's trip back east.

In mid-August, Holiday was back in Chicago, where she opened at Joe Sherman's Garrick Stagebar, along with Henry Red Allen's band. Both band and singer drew enthusiastic crowds; to Sherman's delight, the club was packed every night, and he quickly extended both Allen's and Holiday's contracts until December.

Holiday's seeming good luck did not hold; while being driven to work one evening, her car collided with an ambulance. Suffering cut knees, Holiday asked the driver to take her to the hospital. As the car was leaving, the police arrived at the accident scene and took Holiday into custody for leaving the scene of an accident. Calling Sherman from the police station at first did little; he thought it was all a big joke until Holiday lost her temper and insisted Sherman come to help her. He arrived at the station as soon as he could and posted bail for Holiday. She performed that evening; however, relations with Sherman were forever after strained. Things became even more tense when Holiday learned that Sherman had booked her thinking she was a man. Even though Holiday threatened to quit, the money and the huge number of fans coming to see her mollified her enough to honor her contract and remain until the end of December.

At the same time, Holiday, while performing at the club, with her song list including "Strange Fruit," "God Bless the Child," and "I Cried for You," had moved beyond the artistry of her earlier interpretations and was becoming more stylized, as if playing the same part over every night, until those qualities that made her so unique slid into shadow.

By February 1943, Holiday was back in New York, opening at Kelly's Stables. But much had changed since her last appearance. Her vocals and stylings were no longer fresh. Even her movements and gestures seemed rehearsed rather than spontaneous. Critics who counted themselves fans of Holiday took notice; what they saw saddened them.

By the end of the year, Holiday was back on the West Coast, where her husband was working at an aircraft plant helping with the war effort. Monroe had received time off from his sentence for good behavior. He saw no need to return east or to join his wife. Clearly, the marriage had failed, though Monroe continued to ask for money from Holiday. Yet, although they had gone their separate ways, they did not divorce until 11 years later. Holiday now was seeing many men for dates and casual sex. She was embedded in the same destructive cycle when it came to men that had led her to marry Monroe; while she wanted to remain in control, she also wanted to be controlled, even if it meant having a violent and abusive partner. Each man in her life was called "Daddy"; when the man failed to provide the love or control that she needed, she simply moved on. As men came and went into and out of her life, Holiday was becoming known as a soft touch for those looking to make a fast buck or to get a handout.

At one point, Holiday began a relationship with bass player John Simmons. Years later, Simmons described Holiday as a masochist—that is, someone who enjoys physical pain.[1] Holiday looked for ways to provoke him into hitting her. At one point, he even bought a small whip and beat her with it, taking care not to mar her face. Convinced that she would be unable to perform that evening, Simmons, before he left for his own gig, ran the bathtub full of cold water. He also left a box of salt to treat Holiday's welts. Later that evening as he took a break from performing, Simmons ducked into a club across the street. To his amazement, Holiday was on stage, gardenia in her hair, singing for the audience.

In the middle of July 1943, Holiday was back in New York, performing at another old stomping ground, the Onyx Club on 52nd Street. She remained at the Onyx throughout the rest of 1943 and 1944. The critics were unkind, but perhaps accurate. A reviewer in *Downbeat* stated bluntly: "Billie is not singing at her best."[2] More often than not, Holiday now sang under the influence of several Brandy Alexanders (an alcoholic drink made with brandy, crème de cacao, half-and-half, and grated nutmeg), which caused her to muddy her phrasing and to slur her words. Many fans wondered if Holiday, who was only 28 years old, had already passed her peak.

A SAD NEW CHAPTER

By 1943, life was turning hard for Billie Holiday. Although her popularity was unquestioned, her personal life was unraveling. Not even 30, she had faced numerous obstacles both personally and professionally for most of her life. She remained largely unappreciated, however, and, in many cases, underpaid, considering her talent. Experience had molded Holiday into a woman who spoke her mind and did as she pleased, but it had also left deep wounds that never healed. As a result, she increasingly turned to drugs and alcohol to alleviate her demons.

Never one to shun a good time, Holiday had used marijuana and alcohol since she was a teenager. Holiday loved to go to parties, clubs, and jam sessions, where the drugs were plentiful and the alcohol flowed freely. Even living with Sadie, Holiday had a home life that was one endless house party. During the 1930s, Holiday's use of marijuana and alcohol increased, but she had stayed away from hard drugs such as opium, cocaine, and heroin.

Toward the end of 1943 or early 1944, Holiday crossed the line and began using opium. Many friends blamed James Monroe, who, they believed, introduced Holiday to opium and heroin. Holiday always maintained, though, that Monroe had nothing to do with her turn toward hard drugs. Whether Monroe, who himself smoked opium, influenced her, Holiday began experimenting with opium shortly after her marriage to him.

During the 1930s and 1940s, smoking opium was considered by those of the smart set to be the epitome of "cool." It was a "luxurious vice" to which only a select few could aspire.[3] James Monroe was one of those, and, in part, Holiday's attraction to him was because of his persona: a sharp and flashy hipster who could handle the drug. With the war, however, opium was becoming more difficult to get. To replace it, musicians turned to the more highly addictive and deadly heroin.

Jazz musicians and drugs have always been intertwined. By the early 1940s, many jazz musicians experimented with heroin. Statistics suggest that between 50 and 75 percent of bebop musicians in the 1940s had used heroin; of that number 25 to 33 percent became addicted; almost 20 percent died as a result.[4] Unlike marijuana or alcohol, which often took years to build up dependence, heroin could become addictive in a short period of time. Billie Holiday had seen the ravages of heroin firsthand, making it all the more difficult to understand why she tried it.

By this time, perhaps, Holiday needed an escape that alcohol or marijuana could no longer provide. On the surface, she had a successful career, but because of her unorthodox style, she was still misunderstood. Her accomplishments brought her little satisfaction. She was, despite her many friends and active social life, a very lonely woman. Stinging from the continual snubs and slurs of racism, Holiday was tired, discouraged, and disappointed with her life. The release that heroin promised helped her to cope. Like all addicts, Holiday believed she could control the drug. She ended up another victim. Yet, despite persistent rumors, her addiction remained largely unnoticed until 1945.

A NEW LABEL, ANOTHER NEW START

By 1944, Holiday was still without a record label. She had tried unsuccessfully to re-sign with Columbia. She then contacted Milt Gabler, who had helped to produce "Strange Fruit," and told him she wanted to record again. Gabler was ecstatic; he talked with Joe Glaser and arranged for Holiday to sign a contract with Decca Records, where Gabler was in charge of the pop and jazz A&R (Artist & Repertoire) and of finding and developing new talent. The contract was a good one for Holiday; among other things, she was to receive royalties from her songs for the very first time.

In March 1944, Holiday was back in the studio where, over the course of the next two weeks, she participated in two recording sessions. But even with a new label, the support of Gabler, and a new backup band, Holiday appeared to be going through the motions. Critics panned the results, but Gabler was pleased with the sessions, stating that Billie was in better form than ever before.

Holiday may have been beset by skeptical music critics, money problems, and a worsening drug addiction, but she still had star power. She headed back to the 52nd Street clubs where she made the rounds, always accompanied by her dogs. She also performed on a local New York City radio show. She then went back out on tour, traveling to Chicago to appear at the Grand Terrace, from which years earlier she had been fired. Now she played to standing room–only audiences every night.

Like many jazz vocalists, Billie had a secret desire to record with strings, and, unlike John Hammond, who disliked the idea, Gabler encouraged her to give it a try. It was a battle to get the head of Decca, Jack Kapp, to agree. Gabler was convinced that one of Holiday's standards, "Lover Man," had the potential to be a big hit. He suggested that Holiday rerecord the song, this time with a full orchestra. Gabler's hunch paid off; the new instrumentation added an entirely new dimension to her work. The results were magical.

After her latest session was finished, Holiday returned to 52nd Street, appearing at small clubs such as the Downbeat and the Spotlite. Up-and-coming musicians such as trumpeter Dizzy Gillespie and saxophonist John Coltrane often dropped in to jam with Holiday and the musicians playing with her. For now, the work was steady and jobs were available. Many musicians and jazz writers today believe that Holiday gave her finest live performances during 1943 and 1944.

But Holiday's drug addiction was becoming harder to conceal. She had little trouble getting heroin. As she admitted in her autobiography, "I had the white gowns and the white shoes. And every night they'd bring me the white gardenias and the white junk."[5] In December 1944, Holiday received more bad news; James Monroe had been arrested again for drug smuggling and needed money. Although Holiday still regarded her husband with affection, she could not bring herself to come to his rescue this time.

Part of her reluctance to help Monroe may have arisen because Holiday had a new man in her life: trumpeter Joseph Luke Guy, who had made a name for himself as a solid sideman. Guy was also a drug addict whose drug connections supplied Holiday with heroin. As their relationship intensified, the two began living together, which did not prevent Holiday from seeing other men or women.

1945

On January 17, 1945, Holiday appeared at the Second Annual *Esquire* Magazine Jazz Concert in Los Angeles, where she performed before a sellout crowd of 2,800. She also picked up an award, having been voted "Best Vocalist." After the concert, Holiday performed at a small club. Her appearance was neither announced nor publicized; those fortunate enough to hear her sing "Body and Soul" and "Strange Fruit" gave her a standing ovation. Not long afterward, Holiday's recording of "Lover Man" was released to great acclaim. The Downbeat Club in New York wasted no time. In huge letters on billboards outside the club was the name "Billie Holiday—Opens 22 May."

While still on the West Coast, Holiday began telling people that she had gone to Mexico, where she divorced James Monroe and had married Joe Guy. Friends were skeptical. Details remained sketchy. She also complained of her illness while traveling back to New York, which may have been an allusion to withdrawal symptoms. If there was any question that Billie Holiday was addicted to drugs, it now had been answered.

By the time she returned to New York and began performing at the Downbeat, Holiday was in the throes of her addiction. She began missing shows. Joe Guy was also losing his battle with heroin, and soon after ending his stint with Coleman Hawkins, another up-and-coming trumpeter, Miles Davis from St. Louis, replaced him. Guy may have been out of a job, but he still had a source of money in Holiday, which he tried to get his hands on through a series of ill-conceived business schemes. Regardless of her problems with Guy, Holiday continued to keep an open house at her and Sadie's home in the Bronx. Many people remember Holiday providing meals for those who were unemployed as well as keeping money on hand for subway fare. Many of her friends credited Holiday's generosity for keeping them going as they searched for work or when they needed a place to stay.

Against this background, the jazz scene was also undergoing changes. Big bands were enjoying their last days of popularity. The jazz scene was fracturing into different camps: bebop continued to make inroads, and the first seeds of the sound known as rhythm and blues were beginning to emerge. As Stuart Nicholson pointed out, even with the changes taking place around them, both Holiday and Guy still could have found a musical niche for themselves.[6] That they did not suggests how completely heroin had come to control their lives.

SADIE

As Holiday's name was still a draw, she continued to find work. In late August, after finishing a stint at the McKinley Theater in New York City, Holiday agreed to go on tour with Joe Guy's newly formed band, which included 16 musicians. The idea was that the group would travel and perform a number of one-night shows throughout the South and the Midwest. On September 11, 1945, the band opened in Richmond, Virginia; from there, Holiday and the band made their way to Baltimore, where Holiday was booked to perform at the Royal Theater. On October 6, after finishing their last show, Holiday and Guy returned to their hotel. There Holiday swore that she felt "her mother's spirit come up behind me and put her hand on my shoulder."[7] At this time, Sadie had been quite ill, having suffered a stroke in late September. Holiday learned the next day that her mother was dead. Deeply shaken by her mother's death, Holiday asked Joe Glaser to make the necessary arrangements for the funeral. She then made her way back to New York. On October 9, 1945, a small group of friends gathered to say their goodbyes to Sadie at a funeral mass. Her body was then taken to St. Raymond's Cemetery in the Bronx, where she was interred. It was a day that Holiday never forgot and from which she never recovered.

Sadie's death was a terrible blow. Although their relationship had been stormy, the two women loved each other. Sadie had always been a part of Holiday's life, trying to protect her from the kinds of people who had abused and exploited Sadie. Mother and daughter had struggled to survive hardship, and Sadie had lived to see Billie achieve success as a singer and had, to a certain extent, lived part of her life through her daughter's accomplishments.

In turn, Holiday had done her best to provide her mother with opportunities of her own, such as opening restaurants and making sure she was taken care of. Sadie was a sad figure, battered by life, offering herself as a wounded martyr, abandoned by everyone except her daughter. But she was remembered by many who came to know her as a gentle woman, with a good sense of humor, who had been blessed with the ability to cook. And even though Sadie hounded Billie, argued with her, and, on occasion, embarrassed her, in the end, she was always there for her daughter. With her mother gone, Holiday was an orphan, and she never recovered from her mother's death. For years, when Holiday was drinking, she would succumb to her grief. Remembering the nickname Lester Young had bestowed on Sadie, she cried, "Duchess is gone."[8]

Between her descent into drugs and drink and her deepening loneliness, Holiday became even more dependent in her relationships with men. Her need was so great that she subjected herself to greater abuse and exploitation rather than confront her fears. After her mother's death, Holiday began her long, slow, and painful decline.

NOTES

1. Stuart Nicholson, *Billie Holiday* (Boston: Northeastern University Press, 1995), p. 135.

2. Ibid., p. 133.

3. Ibid., p. 136.

4. Ibid., p. 137.

5. Billie Holiday, with William Dufty, *Lady Sings the Blues* (New York: Doubleday, 1956), p. 116.

6. Nicholson, *Billie Holiday*, p. 145.

7. Holiday, with Dufty, *Lady Sings the Blues*, p. 109.

8. Nicholson, *Billie Holiday*, p. 146.

Chapter 9

JAZZ'S FALLING STAR

In the months following Sadie's death, Holiday fell into a deep depression worsened by her increased drinking and drug use. She could not afford the luxury of doing nothing; she needed to work. Within 24 hours of her mother's funeral, Holiday reluctantly returned to Baltimore on October 10, 1945, to finish her engagement with Joe Guy's band. Less than a week later, she returned to New York. Tired, grieving, and sad, she told Guy that she wanted out of their business venture. By the time the musicians were paid off because of broken contracts and the bills that had accumulated from touring were paid, Holiday was out more than thirty-five thousand dollars, leaving her almost penniless.

Holiday no longer wanted to tour; instead, she preferred to be booked in the small nightclubs and cabarets in New York where she felt more secure and at ease. By the end of October, she was back at the Downtime, where she performed for the rest of the year and into 1946. No matter what shape her voice was in, people still jammed the club to hear her night after night. Holiday also made time to perform at a charity benefit sponsored by the *Amsterdam News,* one of the leading African American newspapers of the period. Despite her reputation as a difficult performer and the toll that her drinking and drug abuse had taken on her voice, Holiday's popularity continued to soar. By the end of 1945, she was 52nd Street's highest paid performer, earning on average one thousand dollars (approximately ten thousand dollars today) a week.

Her drug habit, though, was catching up with her, costing an estimated five hundred dollars a week (approximately fifty-four hundred in today's dollars), prompting Holiday to complain bitterly that she was nothing more than a high-paid slave not only to her employers, but also to the drug. Despite her high salary, Holiday had to borrow money in order to continue buying the drugs that she now needed all the time.

Holiday's ability to consume drugs and alcohol was legendary. One friend later told of how after a show he was invited over to Holiday's house to unwind. Holiday had taken several stimulants to get her through her performance. When she returned home, she smoked some opium, drank, and smoked some marijuana. She then took several pills and drank some more. When she thought nobody was watching, she went to the bathroom to shoot up heroin. Although this lethal combination could have killed her, Holiday continually cheated death. She also never worried about being caught with drugs; a friend held them for her to protect Holiday from charges of possession.

STAYING BUSY

In August 1945, Holiday received the good news that Decca agreed to pick up her contract for another year, with the possibility of an additional 12-month renewal if all went well. During her second year with the company, Holiday recorded eight titles and released four single records. But Holiday's vaunted ability to learn songs quickly was becoming a thing of the past. Milt Gabler noticed that Holiday arrived late for sessions, often unable to begin recording unless she had a glass of brandy to help her voice. Still, Holiday tended to be a one-take singer, so for a while, the expense and headache of endless studio takes were avoided. Things did not go quite as well for her second recording session in January 1946. It was becoming more difficult for Holiday to record in a single take; by the following March, during her third session, Gabler struggled for more than three and a half hours to get one song recorded. Even with these growing problems, the music Holiday recorded during these 1945–1946 sessions at Decca is some of the better work she did for the company.

The success of her records, particularly "Lover Man," brought her a larger audience than ever before, but many of her fans now were not fans of jazz music. Gabler's touch in the studio along with Holiday's talent and style made her more accessible than before. Slowly, Holiday was crossing the line from jazz singer to pop star. With the increased attention, Holiday was also being drawn away from her comfort zone on 52nd Street and into the concert halls. By 1946, she had already performed in two concerts along with several other jazz singers and musicians. Managers were clamoring for Holiday to perform alone in a concert setting, something no jazz singer had ever done before.

Certainly notable among her solo concert appearances was her debut on February 16, 1946, at the New York Town Hall, where she played to a sold-out house. Although nervous, Holiday gave a top-notch performance and was rewarded by enthusiastic applause. It was a personal triumph, one that was long overdue in light of her contributions to the music world. Those who knew Holiday and her music more intimately, however, saw the concert as one-dimensional, with most of the songs played at the same tempo, with little variation in her phrasing. It was by all accounts almost technically perfect, but devoid of emotion or depth.

The popular success of the Town Hall concert, however, convinced Holiday to take more chances outside the nightclub venue. On April 4, 1946, she appeared at a Carnegie Hall benefit concert alongside some of the country's top folk singers such as Pete Seeger and Woody Guthrie. Three days later, on April 7, to celebrate her 31st birthday, Holiday gave a concert at the McKinley Gardens in Brooklyn to an enthusiastic audience. She wrapped up the month by giving two more concerts—one at the Apollo, the other at Eaton Hall. Each time she found a receptive audience, despite her erratic performances.

NEW ORLEANS

It seemed now that everyone was interested in Billie Holiday. In September 1946, Holiday was on a plane headed to Hollywood to record the soundtrack for the upcoming United Artists Picture, *New Orleans*. The studio had seen the success that MGM had with its African American singers such as Lena Horne and Ethel Waters. Hoping to cash in on the trend, United Artists lined up a cast that included not only Billie Holiday, but also Louis Armstrong. Rumor had it that United Artists had dispatched a secondary film crew to New Orleans to shoot footage of an African American funeral and street parade.

The story was set against the backdrop of the closing of the notorious New Orleans red-light district Storyville, where jazz got its start. Many hoped that for the first time a film would portray the story of jazz as honestly as possible. Given the cast, it seemed that United Artists might succeed where other studios had not.

But what had been put to paper never made it to film. Instead, the story focused on the romantic troubles of a young white opera singer played by Dorothy Patrick and her decision about whether to give up her career and run away with a gambler, played by Arturo de Cordova. Holiday's role was that of a maid to Patrick's character. Though she carried off the part gracefully, she was seething inside. Having vowed as a young girl that she would never clean houses for anybody, Holiday found the role demeaning. It was a cruel irony that, at the height of her stardom, Hollywood relegated Holiday to a stereotypical role.

There were other problems, too. A strong wave of anti-Communist fervor was sweeping the country, spearheaded by Senator Joseph McCarthy and his far-reaching efforts to ferret out suspected members of, or sympathizers with, the Communist Party. McCarthy aimed part of his investigation at Hollywood, where a number of people working in the film and television industry had earlier flirted with Communism or other left-wing causes. McCarthyism hit *New Orleans* particularly hard because both the producer and the writer had at first refused to turn the film's African American characters into the prevailing stereotypes. Fearful of the potential consequences that such defiance would bring, the studio heads put enough pressure on the filmmakers that, in the end, Holiday and most of the other black actors were relegated to traditional roles. After a hasty finish and a very limited run, the studio withdrew the picture from circulation

Amid this turmoil, Holiday had troubles of her own. Joe Guy had come from New York to bring Holiday drugs. When he arrived on the movie set, Joe Glaser had him banned. Holiday then paid for Guy to fly back to New York. But her secret was out; not only was she continually late to the studio, causing production to go into costly overtime, but she did not have the necessary discipline to act in films. It was an unfortunate end to her film career; she would never be asked again to appear in a movie. She returned to New York and to the Downtime Club, which now billed her as "America's No. 1 Song Stylist." Her return, however, did not bring in the crowds as before; the war was over, and 52nd Street was changing. No longer was the street a magnet for the clubgoers and the elite; instead, strip clubs and low-rent bars were appearing. Business was so slow that the management at the Downtime, having had to let go of her backup band, also gave Holiday the bad news that she was taking a pay cut.

CONFRONTING THE DEMONS

Nineteen forty-seven started on a brighter note when Holiday appeared in the annual *Downbeat* magazine's popularity poll at number two, the same spot she had held the year before. She was as popular as ever and still in demand; when not performing at the Downtime, she appeared at Carnegie Hall as a surprise guest at a Louis Armstrong concert in February. Then in April, she again appeared with Armstrong at the premiere of *New Orleans* in the Crescent City. When she returned to New York, she learned that the Downtime had decided to shut down until the summer when business would pick up again.

Now that Holiday was between jobs, her manager, Joe Glaser, decided it was time to confront Holiday about her drug addiction. By this time, Holiday was spending almost all of her money buying drugs. Things had gotten so bad that Holiday began asking for advances on her booking fees; when an engagement ended, she was never sure how much money she had coming. When she ran out of her own funds, she borrowed from friends. Besides trying to get Holiday clean of drugs, Glaser also wanted to step in between Holiday and Joe Guy, whom he saw as a freeloader and a troublemaker.

In February 1947, Glaser gave her an ultimatum: seek treatment for her addiction or he would drop her as a client. Holiday reluctantly agreed. In mid-March 1947, she checked into a private hospital in Westchester, New York, to try to kick heroin. By now, her addiction was so acute that at the first sign of withdrawal, Holiday immediately shot herself full of heroin. She had long passed the point at which heroin provided her pleasure; she used just to dull the pain, just to feel normal, or to feel numb. Although she stayed in the hospital for six weeks, when she left, nothing really had changed. Holiday still could see no reason to stop using drugs, and seems not to have wanted to. Between the business of making a living and the malignant presence of Joe Guy, the pressure on Holiday was overwhelming. Glaser tried to hire her an assistant to keep the drug dealers and Guy away, but any hope he had of his client staying clean soon faded.

Not long after her release from the hospital, Holiday was back at work, appearing at the Onyx Club. Then, with Joe Guy, her accompanist Bobby Tucker, her road manager Jimmy Ascendio, and a chauffeur, she headed for her next job, a week-long engagement at the Earle Theater in Philadelphia. The group checked into the Attucks Hotel. Everything seemed to go well until the last night. As usual, her chauffeur came to pick her up, along with Tucker and Ascendio, for the ride back to the hotel. Unknown to them, federal narcotics agents were waiting for Holiday to arrive. Ascendio and Tucker entered the hotel and went to Holiday's room to pack; Holiday remained in the car. When the agents asked for permission to search the room, Tucker and Ascendio granted it. In the course of the search, an agent discovered a spoon, needles, and drugs, including heroin, concealed inside a woman's stocking. Holiday wasted no time. She told the chauffeur to head back to New York immediately. She contacted Joe Glaser, who told her to go to the police, thinking he could use his influence to save Holiday from a long jail sentence. Holiday refused.

At five o'clock in the morning, three days after she fled Philadelphia, the New York City police arrested Holiday at her home. She agreed to accompany the officers to the Grampion Hotel, where she kept a room solely to do drugs; at the time, Joe Guy was staying there. When the police arrived, Guy tried to escape through an open window but was caught and arrested. The police took Holiday and Guy to the New York offices of the Federal Bureau of Narcotics and turned them over to federal narcotics agents. There, under intense questioning and with no legal representation, Holiday admitted that the drugs found at the Attucks belonged to her. She was charged with drug possession and released. That evening, Holiday was performing at a small club on 52nd Street. Later that night, she and Bobby Tucker went to Carnegie Hall, where she made a guest appearance at a jazz concert. Despite the terrible ordeal she had faced earlier in the day, she gave a masterful performance.

Three days after her appearance at Carnegie Hall, Holiday was in court, where on Glaser's instruction, she waived her right to a lawyer. Instead, she pled guilty to one count of receiving and concealing narcotics and asked that she be sent to a hospital for treatment. Waiving her right to legal representation turned out to be the biggest mistake Holiday could have made. Glaser mistakenly assumed that the court would be lenient, and since Holiday's drug offense was minor, the punishment would fit the crime. Advising her to waive her right to counsel was his way of forcing Holiday to enter a rehabilitation program to get the help she so desperately needed. The judge had other ideas. He sentenced Holiday to one year in jail to be served at the Federal Reformatory for Women in Alderson, West Virginia. Holiday suffered another devastating blow from which she never fully recovered.

Holiday might have escaped jail time if she had had legal representation. Although the prosecution contended that the drugs found in the Attucks Hotel were Holiday's, they failed to connect either Holiday or Joe Guy directly to them. They had no evidence except Holiday's admission, which a clever lawyer could have argued was coerced and thus inadmissible. Ironically, when the same evidence was presented at Guy's trial, and Guy admitted under oath that he had bought drugs for Holiday, the jury acquitted him. As Holiday prepared to leave for prison, she must have wondered how the man who introduced her to heroin and was in part responsible for her addiction could be set free, while she was sent to jail.

BEHIND BARS

On May 28, 1947, Billie Holiday stepped off the train and was taken to the prison. Upon arrival, she was admitted to the prison hospital, where over the course of the next few days, she suffered from weakness, anxiety, and nausea. To help ease the pain of withdrawal, she was periodically given a small dose of morphine. Her prison medical records suggest that Holiday did not go through a terribly difficult withdrawal period, in part because of her previous stay at the Westchester hospital, where her tolerance to heroin had been somewhat reduced. After eight days, Holiday was well enough to leave the hospital and be placed in the general prison population. She was given a light workload, which consisted of cleaning brass. She preferred to work alone and did her duties conscientiously. In her spare time, she sewed and played cards. While in prison, Holiday never made any reference to her career. That did not prevent some inmates from recognizing her; Holiday, in turn, was gracious, kind, and happy to be surrounded by fans. She spoke eagerly of returning to work; she worried lest the public forget her.

During her time in prison, Holiday became good friends with Helen Hironimus, the prison warden. In Hironimus, Holiday found someone who was helpful, understanding, and sympathetic to her troubles. Holiday trusted Hironimus enough to turn over her affairs to her, which included answering fan mail and responding to inquiries from magazines and radio stations. Hironimus became especially concerned about the state of Holiday's finances. She even wrote to the IRS to protect Holiday from prosecution for failure to pay back taxes.

Hironimus's intervention was all the more necessary because Joe Glaser abandoned Holiday during her imprisonment. She wrote him repeatedly, asking him to visit, send money, and launch a publicity campaign. Glaser ignored her letters and did nothing. In August, he did send fifty dollars and promised to send more, but additional money never arrived. Hironimus at last stepped in, asking Glaser to send her an account of Holiday's finances.

In response, Glaser stated only that Holiday owed his office $715.29, telling Hironimus that Holiday had squandered more than one hundred thousand dollars in the last two years, largely because of her drug use. When a benefit concert for Holiday was scheduled with the proceeds going to pay her expenses, Glaser intervened, saying that Holiday did not need the money. By the end of 1947, Holiday had had enough and decided to switch agents; she contacted the Ed Fishman Agency, asking if Fishman would represent her. Hironimus also wrote Fishman, explaining the difficulties with Glaser. Fishman agreed to take on Holiday as a client. When Glaser heard the news, he refused to return Holiday's wardrobe and tried to intimidate her to stay with him. Aware of the kind of tactics Glaser might use, Fishman advised Holiday to sit tight.

In December 1947, Holiday was eligible for parole; however, Hironimus suggested that Holiday serve out her sentence, as doing so would give her a few more months to make sure she was ready to face the world drug-free. Holiday agreed. On March 16, 1948, Holiday was released from prison and remained on parole until May 27, 1948. One condition of her parole was that she live with Bobby Tucker and his mother while she got back on her feet. In the meantime, Glaser still refused to turn over accounting records or to release Holiday as a client. Hironimus wrote to Glaser again, angrily asking him why he was being so difficult at a time when Holiday needed support to stay clean and pick up the pieces of her life and career.

It made little difference; even as Holiday was preparing to settle in with the Tuckers, Glaser was maneuvering to keep her as a client. Holiday did little to help herself. Fishman later told Hironimus that Holiday had fired him in order to stay with Glaser. The reason for the sudden switch was the reappearance of Holiday's husband James Monroe, who had returned to New York City and who urged Holiday to keep Glaser on. At one point while in prison, Holiday told Fishman that if she had to stay with Glaser, she would stop singing forever. Holiday was back with an agent who showed little concern for her well-being, but she was broke and she needed work.

A COMEBACK CONCERT

Less than two weeks after Holiday's discharge from prison, on March 16, 1948, she was scheduled to sing at Carnegie Hall. As soon as tickets were available, there was a mad rush at the box office; 2,700 seats were sold in advance, more than those sold for Stan Kenton, who was the biggest draw in jazz in 1948. There was some confusion, though, about who represented Holiday, as the concert promoter found himself dealing with both Glaser and Fishman. In the end, Glaser made the arrangements for his client.

On the night of the concert, hundreds stood in the rain with the hope of buying tickets to the hottest show in town. When she arrived backstage, Holiday was nervous, excited, and clean. As she made her way on stage, the hall erupted in spontaneous applause. Holiday then sang her way into the audience's hearts. If she had fears about being forgotten, they instantly dissolved. Following no set program, Holiday, backed up by a small quartet led by Bobby Tucker, sang from her repertoire; her voice was clear and steady. With each round of applause, her eyes showed her gratitude. Although she appeared relaxed and rested, the hard reality was that her drug use had begun to ravage her appearance; her face was puffy, and she looked older than her 33 years. Encouraged by the response to her return, her agent booked Holiday for another concert in three weeks. This time she broke her own box office record of a few weeks before.

Despite her successful comeback, Holiday faced another problem: acquiring the necessary cabaret card to perform in nightclubs. In New York City, anyone wishing to perform at a nightclub or cabaret needed a special permit before being allowed on stage. But because of her drug conviction, Holiday was denied the permit. Even though she was free to perform at concert halls and theaters, she was legally banned from singing at nightclubs that sold alcohol. In exasperation, she exclaimed, "I can play Carnegie, but I can't play the crummiest gin joint in New York."[1]

Holiday was now scrambling to find work. Unexpected help came from Al Wilde, a Broadway producer who wanted Holiday for a revue he was organizing. Almost a month after her first comeback concert at Carnegie Hall, Billie Holiday was starring on Broadway in "Holiday on Broadway." The show earned good reviews but closed after only five days because of lack of publicity. At the same time, Holiday formally gave notice to Fishman that she was staying with Joe Glaser. Her decision was another bad one; after trying so hard to get away from the people who had let her down after her arrest, she was right back where she started. Any chance of staying free of drugs was rapidly disappearing.

Shortly after her Broadway run ended, Holiday met another man who offered to help her. Co-owner of the Club Ebony, located at 1678 Broadway, John Levy told her that if she sang at his club, he could get her a necessary cabaret card. A balding, overweight businessman known for his taste in beautiful women, Levy had come to show business through retailing. By many accounts, he was disliked for his controlling ways and poor treatment of the workers at his club. Bobby Tucker once described him as a "pimp, an awful person," but that did not stop Holiday from becoming involved with him. She was eager for work and for companionship. She agreed to Levy's proposition and in early May began performing under a four-week contract. Her appearances became the biggest attraction in New York clubs. Holiday also worked hard to overcome her bad reputation: she showed up on time and performed every night. Her popularity was so great that she had to beg to leave the stage when she finished her set. Although grateful for the opportunity and support she received, Holiday never stopped complaining. She often grumbled, for example, that people only came to see her to glimpse the track marks on her arms. She vowed to outwit and disappoint them by wearing long gloves. Her success at the Ebony led to radio appearances and additional bookings at the Strand Theater, where she drew the largest crowds seen there in years.

Still, self-doubt plagued her; it seemed everywhere she turned, her actions were carefully watched. She was under constant scrutiny from the police, who were ready to arrest her if they spotted drugs on her. Because of this constant harassment, many of Holiday's friends began to avoid her, concerned about their own reputations.

John Levy had his eye on Holiday for other reasons. He bought her an expensive Cadillac and gave her gifts, all the time telling her that she would be better off if he were her manager. Soon he was controlling all of Holiday's finances. When she asked for the money she had earned performing at his club, Levy withheld it, telling her that he would give her what she needed and hold on to the rest. In the meantime, Levy was spending the money. Despite his abusive treatment, Holiday stayed with him. She complained that Levy "makes me wait on him, not him on me.... I never do anything without John telling me."[2] Yet, her dependency on Levy was so great that she submitted to cruel mental and physical abuse. Levy took full advantage of Holiday's fragile emotional state and drug addiction, using both to control her. There was nothing anyone could do to end the relationship. To her great sorrow, Holiday's relationship with Levy landed her in trouble again.

In January 1949, Levy and Holiday were in San Francisco, where she was performing. From the beginning, the trip was a disaster. After finishing her last show, Holiday stepped into the kitchen where she and some of her fans gathered to talk and drink. At some point, Holiday complained to Levy that one of the customers was getting fresh with her. Levy wasted no time. He grabbed a butcher knife and tried to stab the offender. Levy missed and wounded a bystander in the shoulder, who stumbled out onto the stage with the knife protruding. Holiday got into the fracas, throwing plates, cups, and other kitchenware at those in the kitchen. The incident landed three people in the hospital; both Levy and Holiday were arrested but later released on bail.

The incident actually proved a boon to the club owners who had booked Holiday; she played to crowded rooms, filled with fans and the curious. Holiday's troubles were compounded when, two weeks later, she was arrested again for possession of narcotics. While in their hotel room, Levy received a call warning him that narcotics agents were on their way to arrest him. Levy then gave Holiday all of his drugs, telling her to get rid of them. But before she could do anything, agents entered the room and arrested the two of them for possession. Levy beat the charges and left town, abandoning Holiday to deal with the courts on her own. Having learned her lesson the hard way, Holiday got a lawyer and maintained that she had been framed. She was acquitted of the drug charges, but the damage had been done. Her reputation suffered another setback, and she was struggling financially. She could not even pay her legal fees because Levy had spent her money.

Holiday continued to struggle throughout the rest of 1948 and 1949 to regain her footing. But by now, she had relapsed. The few recording sessions she did became nightmares, as she failed to show up or could not always perform if she did. Although her bookings increased for live performances, Holiday could not stick to her resolution to act profession- ally. Even the opportunity of performing with her idol Louis Armstrong in late 1949 did not help. Holiday was slipping—and, perhaps worse, she knew it.

NOTES

1. Billie Holiday, with William Dufty, *Lady Sings the Blues* (New York: Doubleday, 1956), p. 148.

2. Billie Holiday, interview, *Ebony*, July 1949.

Chapter 10

THE SPOTLIGHT DIMS

In 1950, Billie Holiday was 35 years old. She appeared to be at the peak of her singing career, but continuous money problems, involvement in another destructive love affair, and drug addiction were taking a heavy toll. For the last five years, her personal life had gradually overshadowed her professional accomplishments. Although she was still much in demand as a performer, her professional reputation lay in tatters, marred by her inconsistent and erratic behavior.

Scandal dogged her. She was, for instance, named in several lawsuits. Edward Fishman, who had tried valiantly to rescue Holiday from Joe Glaser, was now suing her for seventy-five thousand dollars for breach of contract. A woman who was wounded in the bar fracas in San Francisco was also suing her. On a brief tour with a Los Angeles band, Holiday ran into some undisclosed trouble in South Carolina, which left her without money. Wiring Levy for money, she promised to send for the band when she got back to Los Angeles. Band members waited in vain; she never sent for them. After repeated attempts to settle the matter failed, the band appealed to the musicians' union for help and threatened legal action against Holiday as a last resort.

Beset by legal problems, Holiday learned at the same time that Levy had committed her to a number of contracts without her knowledge. To her credit, Holiday honored those commitments; then one night while performing in Washington, D.C., she ran away from Levy. The 18-month relationship was over; Holiday was almost broke but at least she had gotten free of Levy, who had squandered thousands of dollars gambling and purchasing a home.

After her split from Levy, though, Holiday's downward spiral continued. She walked out on a job after only three days, without being paid for
the performance she had given, which, given her financial woes, she could
ill afford to do. She had yet to pay the lawyer who represented her at her
second drug trial, who now began to press her. To add to her troubles, her
chauffeur was picked up on a drug charge, and her new blue Lincoln Con-
tinental was impounded. She was media fodder, but she drew in crowds,
and club owners and promoters were still willing to hire her.

By now Holiday's life had been reduced to traveling from job to job,
trying to make enough money to buy the drugs she needed for the day.
Anita O'Day, a singer who appeared with Holiday at a series of dates in
Los Angeles and herself a heroin addict, recalled:

> I wasn't only in awe of her singing, I was in awe of her habit.
> She didn't cook up on a spoon ... [Heroin is watered down in a
> spoon and then "cooked" by holding a lighter or match under
> it.] she used a small tuna can and shot 10 cc into her feet. Later
> ... she ran out of veins.[1]

Drugs and alcohol continued to take their toll. Her voice at times was
raw and haggard; gone was the melodic instrument that had captivated
so many. Her performances became more and more erratic; she was often
late for shows and high when she performed. There were times when she
simply did not show up. Her recording sessions were few and equally erratic. Holiday herself admitted that her life was spinning out of control.
But in the early months of 1951, life seemed to take a turn for the better
when she met a new man, Louis McKay.

ANOTHER NEW START

At first, Louis McKay hardly seemed like the kind of man Holiday
might be drawn to. He was no Jimmy Monroe or John Levy, no slick
hustler or low-life character. Though other accounts vary, McKay stated
that he first met Holiday when she and Sadie were living in Harlem. He
became friends with Sadie, who asked McKay if he would help her keep
an eye on Billie. McKay also stated that he and Holiday had dated a little,
but this claim has never been verified.

The truth seems to be that Holiday met McKay in 1951 while performing at a club in Detroit where McKay was the manager. According
to McKay, Holiday had sought him out, asking for help and threaten-
ing suicide if he refused. In an interview after Holiday's death, McKay

recalled: "I told her that I wouldn't leave my job in Detroit and abandon my obligations there, until she was ready to kick her drug habit. I refused to go on the road with her until this was done."[2] Although many found McKay to be weak and a fool, it did appear that he made Holiday serious about cleaning up her drug habit, despite using drugs himself. At one point, she spoke of retiring in order to be a housewife and take care of McKay. Others saw a difference in her performances; she was singing better and appeared more organized and responsible.

In 1951, Holiday moved to the West Coast. There she could perform freely and not have to worry about getting a cabaret card. Though she still found steady work, she was without a recording contract. She had agreed to make some records for Aladdin Recording Company, but neither side was terribly interested in pursuing the deal. Holiday especially feared that, because of the company's poor record of distribution, she would lose her audience. She talked about the problem with Joe Glaser, who in turn spoke with his West Coast representative for Aladdin, who agreed to talk to Norman Granz. Among the leading jazz promoters, Granz had worked with Holiday in the past and was excited at the prospect of working with her again.

In 1952, she signed a recording contract with Granz. For the first time in many years, Holiday felt secure; she knew firsthand from working with him that Granz cared about musicians and took care to treat them fairly. Granz was aware of Holiday's troubles, particularly with her voice, which continued to grow throatier; she no longer had a high range to work with, which made arranging her songs a challenge. But Granz also recognized that Holiday was still capable of conveying an emotional intensity in her singing.

One of the first things Granz did in the studio was to try to move Holiday from the comfort zone of her songbook. Granz allowed her to record a few of her favorites, but also insisted that Holiday sing songs that challenged her. As nervous as his efforts made her, she tried to do as Granz asked because she realized he was doing what John Hammond had figured out years earlier: pushing her to reach a higher level of performance than she thought she could attain. Nevertheless, the sessions were a struggle; Holiday's voice was in such bad shape that at times she was forced to speak the lyrics instead of singing them. Still, there was a maturity and sadness that permeated her songs, as if the last several years of her life had allowed her to ascend to an emotional level that she might not have achieved years earlier. The fruits of Granz's efforts paid off with the release of *Billie Holiday Sings*, just in time for the 1952 Christmas season, earning Holiday some of the best reviews she'd had in years. Holiday continued working with Granz for the next five years, until just before her death. He recognized something that many had overlooked: no matter the trouble or despair in her life, Holiday simply needed to sing.

Despite her performances with some of the greatest jazz performers in the country, her sold-out concerts, and a hit record, Holiday hit roadblocks; earlier that year, a planned television special featuring Holiday was cancelled because her scrapes with the law and messy personal life frightened the network executives. Perhaps even more frustrating, Holiday still could not get a cabaret license in New York City; as a result, her earning power was severely decreased as well as her exposure to the New York music scene. Instead, Glaser continued to book Holiday at other top spots in Chicago, Boston, Los Angeles, and San Francisco, where she commanded top dollar.

After years of negative publicity, Holiday finally got a chance to tell her side of the story with an appearance on the popular television program "Comeback." The program chronicled the life stories of people who had come back from some type of adversity, such as illness or catastrophe. Although Holiday fit well within the theme of the program, she was an extreme example of the people the program normally featured.

Holiday spoke frankly about her life, leaving very little out. She talked about segregation, racism, and her prison term, shocking topics by the standards of that time. Even more startling was her admission of her drug addiction. Interspersed with Holiday's narrative were stories of people whom she had known and with whom she had worked, such as Count Basie and Artie Shaw. Songs from her recordings were played, and Holiday performed "God Bless the Child." The live performance suffered, as Holiday was recuperating from dental surgery, but it did not lessen the impact of her story or her voice.

In part, Holiday's rebound can be attributed to Louis McKay, who had brought a measure of stability to her life. He was serious about helping her overcome her addiction and made a point to discourage anyone who tried to sell or give Holiday drugs. Not everything was rosy between the couple, though. Like Levy, McKay used Holiday's drug addiction to control her. He was also spending her money on himself to buy, among other things, a house and a share of a nightclub in Chicago, where he promised Holiday a job singing for several months every year. But like so many of the promises other men had made to her, this one also proved false.

EUROPE BOUND

In late December 1953, Joe Glaser and a Swedish promoter signed contracts that would take Holiday to Europe, where she would be the headline performer in a series of shows called *Jazz Club USA*. When told the news, Holiday was ecstatic; going to Europe had been a longtime dream, and she knew that a strong and loyal fan base was there waiting for her. As soon as all the arrangements were made, Holiday would set sail on January 7, 1954. But there were still problems to contend with: Holiday had no passport, and she did not have a birth certificate necessary to apply for one. Yet, for once, arrangements fell into place. She managed to retrieve a copy of her birth certificate, and prepared to depart for Europe.

The first concert was held in Stockholm, Sweden. It did not go well; the musicians were tired from lack of sleep, as well as dealing with transportation problems and the inclement weather. Holiday was not at her best either, having spent part of the previous evening arguing with Leonard Feather, a music writer who had agreed to take on the role of Holiday's assistant. To make matters worse, a hypodermic needle was found in Holiday's dressing room after the show. At first there was talk of sending Holiday back to the United States, but Red Norvo, one of the bandleaders on the tour, made a strong case, citing Holiday's lack of sleep and tension over the show. It was agreed that Holiday could stay. On the second night of their tour, she reportedly sang like a bird.

Everywhere she went in Europe, Holiday was treated like royalty. Nightly bouquets of flowers became the norm; she was thronged by enthusiastic autograph-seekers and was in demand for interviews and radio appearances. It was a sharp contrast to the treatment she received back home, where her visitors generally consisted of drug dealers and hangers-on. The tour was grueling, but Holiday for the most part reveled in the journey. There were mood swings and arguments; at one point Holiday threatened to leave, but with McKay there to support her, she stayed the course. In February, Holiday was scheduled to perform at London's great Albert Hall. While she was in the city, a young English music writer named Michael Brooks accompanied another reporter to interview Holiday. A big fan of Holiday's, Brooks was beside himself with anticipation at the thought of meeting one of his idols. Years later in 1991, when compiling liner notes for a collection of Billie Holiday's recordings, Brooks wrote:

> I don't remember very much of the interview, except that it (naturally) centered around drugs, with Billie vouchsafing that she was clean and had been for some considerable time. My memory of her was that of a big, raw-boned woman [who] seemed incredibly tired and [whose] speech trailed off towards the end of the sentences, while her eyes, which seemed to have difficulty focusing.[3]

That night Holiday sang before an audience of 6,000 people, the largest before which she had ever performed. The crowd's enthusiastic and heart-felt response to Holiday was among the greatest moments of her life.

"LADY YESTER-DAY"

Early spring found Billie back in the United States, where, still without a cabaret license, she was forced to sing at seedy clubs to make a living. She was becoming increasingly frustrated with her situation, as she was still a top draw at concerts held in Carnegie Hall and other top-notch theaters. Gone too were the screaming fans; her dressing room was darkened again by the pushers, pimps, and hustlers looking for a handout. She returned to the recording studio, where Granz hoped to make another record. The session was cut short when Granz realized that Holiday, who had been drinking heavily, was in no condition to continue.

Better news arrived in the summer of 1954 when Holiday was asked to perform for the first Newport Jazz Festival in Newport, Rhode Island, an annual festival that is still held today. Some 13,000 people braved the rain to attend the first night's performance, which featured Holiday. Covered in everything from raincoats to picnic blankets to shower curtains, the crowd roared when Holiday stepped onstage. That evening, she sang accompanied by some of the greatest names in jazz, including Teddy Wilson, Oscar Peterson, George Shearing, and Dizzy Gillespie. The event also reunited Holiday with Lester Young, whom she had not spoken to since 1951, when the two quarreled over her drug use. Their appearance brought a standing ovation from the crowd; whatever rift that had occurred was completely healed. Holiday earned further recognition that year with *Downbeat*'s naming her one of the "great all-time vocalists in jazz."[4] It seemed that Holiday was finally getting the notice and recognition she deserved for her many contributions to jazz.

Prodded by McKay, Holiday considered collaborating with writer William Dufty on an autobiography. Up to this point, she had shied away from earlier requests, telling reporters that her life was such that it could not be printed for others to read. Some have suggested, though, that the reason Holiday held out was from her embarrassment at lacking a formal education. She finally agreed, and, in November 1956, *Lady Sings the Blues* was published. The book, stated Holiday biographer Stuart Nicholson in 1995, "has been the bane of writers ever since."[5]

By the time Holiday and Dufty sat down to write the book, enough time had passed for Holiday to forget or become confused about many of the people, places, and events in her life, in part because of her drug use, which impaired her memory. Dufty seemed unfazed by the problems, and when a gap in her life history appeared, he simply made up facts or embellished the truth. The result was a book that has made it extremely difficult to nail down the truths and falsehoods about Holiday's life. Somehow, though, Holiday's essence was in the book, as she presented herself as a woman battered by love and by life. It was a hard-luck story to be sure, but Holiday's resilience and strength remained alive in the pages. She may have been a victim, but she was also a survivor.

While at work on the book throughout 1955 as well as singing, Holiday found time to return to the studio under Granz's supervision. The results were mixed; heavy smoking left Holiday with smoker's cough and a persistent hoarseness and also affected her breathing. Throughout the sessions, her voice was harsh and uncertain, prompting *Downbeat* to call her "Lady Yester-Day."[6] On stage, it was becoming more apparent that Holiday was struggling. As musical styles changed, she seemed trapped by the past, refusing to bring new songs into her live shows. Worse, her refusal to budge from her standard repertoire on stage had turned her act into Billie Holiday performing as a caricature of Billie Holiday. For those around her, her decline was tragic.

CLOSING CURTAINS

The remaining years of Billie Holiday's life were clouded with sadness, grief, and trouble. Her dependence on heroin had diminished to some extent, but to make up for her need for drugs, she began drinking more heavily. She was rapidly becoming a shadow of her former self. In late February 1956, she was back in the headlines when she and McKay were arrested in Philadelphia for drug possession during an early morning raid on their hotel room. Along with drug paraphernalia, the police also found a small amount of cocaine and heroin that the couple had been using to shoot "speedballs." Although they were released from jail after only a short time, the affair scared Holiday enough to convince her to check into a clinic to get clean. This time, rather than completely weaning Holiday off heroin, doctors administered a combination of different drugs to help manage her gradual withdrawal. Although they seemed to work initially, the drugs could not compensate for the heroin, and upon her release, Holiday turned to alcohol. She managed to stay clear of heroin for a while, but she came to depend on alcohol to rescue her from her pain, just as she once relied on heroin.

By mid-March, she was on the road. But Holiday was beginning to lose her grip. The constant traveling was wearing her down. More bookings placed her in second-class spots; in some cases, she might be booked at one of the high-level clubs only with the understanding that she would perform at other venues owned by club managers. After many years of watching her self-destruct, owners and managers were less likely to take a chance on her; her voice was deteriorating; physically, she was a wreck; and she was rumored to be drinking up to two or three bottles of gin or vodka a day. Then there was the concern over whether Holiday would even show up to perform. Still, Holiday continued to make the rounds, picking up club dates wherever she could, often zigzagging back and forth across the country to perform. When she did appear on stage, she often had to be helped to the microphone. She forgot lyrics and sometimes just looked lost.

In early 1957, Holiday and McKay were called back to Philadelphia, where they were to stand trial for drug charges. In order to keep each other from testifying, the couple decided to marry as soon as Holiday could obtain a divorce from Jimmy Monroe. On March 28, 1957, in Chihuahua, Mexico, they were wed. A year later, they were found guilty and sentenced to a yearlong probation; the judge also warned both that they had to register with the police anytime either of them came to Philadelphia.

By now there was little love between the two; McKay clearly gained more from the marriage than did Holiday. Not only did he have access to her money, but he was now seeing other women. He often made fun of his wife and her troubles; at other times, he physically abused her. Most of the time, Holiday was too sick and disoriented to fight back. After the trial, the couple separated; the following year, Holiday filed for divorce, but never followed through.

Prior to her leaving McKay, Holiday became involved with a shady lawyer, Earle Warren Zaidins. Although Zaidins had no show business background, he promised that he could collect the royalty money due to Holiday from her recordings. He promised that Holiday did not have to pay him unless he won her case. He gradually gained Holiday's confidence, and she began using him as her lawyer.

It proved to be another disastrous decision. Not only did Zaidins keep Holiday supplied with drugs but he also began making romantic overtures toward her. With McKay out of the picture, Zaidins took his place as Holiday's manager. His lack of knowledge about the music business had catastrophic consequences. When a dispute arose between Holiday and the manager of the Apollo, Holiday told Zaidins to sue. Instead of cautioning and restraining Holiday, he allowed the situation to escalate. Keeping good relations with the theater was essential to Holiday's earnings, for it was one of the few places in New York where she could perform. In the end, the owner of the Apollo apologized to Holiday. But the damage had been done: Holiday would never again be asked back.

By now, Holiday had retreated far from the world. Holed up in a tiny ground floor apartment, she remained hidden. Her daily routine consisted of watching television, drinking, and smoking. When she could, she slept. Her only attachment by that time was her beloved Chihuahua Pepi, whom she carried with her everywhere.

LADY IN SATIN

On February 18, 1958, Holiday returned to Columbia Records, the company for which she had made her first recording to do what would be her last. She was scheduled to work three sessions. Her producer this time was Ray Ellis, whom Holiday requested because of his masterful ability at using strings. Unlike her sessions with Norman Granz, Holiday this time wanted to do songs she had not sung before. Ellis agreed and the two went down the street to a local record store and looked at sheet music. Thumbing through the sheet music, Holiday picked out the lyrics she enjoyed the most. Ellis later recalled how he watched Holiday pick her material, not realizing at the time that she was choosing songs that reflected her life, such as "You've Changed," "End of a Love Affair," and "Glad to Be Unhappy." The result was the release of what many consider to be Holiday's most controversial album, *Lady in Satin*.

Many fans found the album too painful to listen to. It was as if Holiday was chronicling her life story, singing it in a voice that was worn out and used up. Ray Ellis's arrangements did not help much; the background seems too lush, contrived, and artificial against the raw pain of Holiday's voice. But others found the album to be as honest and real a collection of songs as Holiday was capable of producing. She had come full circle; starting at Columbia as an ambitious and fresh new voice, she now returned, worn down but wiser.

Later in the year, Holiday ventured to Europe twice to play a series of dates, but she was poorly received. The tours were plagued in part because of Earle Zaidins's bungling of travel arrangements and inept contracts. Yet Holiday returned to the United States in a hopeful mood. She traveled to Monterey, California, where she appeared before a large crowd of 6,000 for a jazz festival. Still, her appearance did little to disguise her worsening condition.

In early March 1959, Holiday walked into the Columbia studios for the last time. She was again working with Ray Ellis. This time, to make sure she made it to her sessions, a nurse was hired. During the sessions, Holiday sat on a barstool. The nurse was always close by in case Holiday lost her balance and started to fall. The nurse also helped her to the bathroom and in general saw to it that Holiday was as comfortable as possible. Holiday's efforts culminated in the album *Billie Holiday*. It bore sad testimony to Holiday's continuing decline as an artist.

A FINAL BLOW

On March 15, 1959, Holiday's soulmate and confidante, Lester Young, died. His death took a severe toll on Holiday, and her grief knew no bounds. The two had traveled a magical musical journey together. His death was a sad reminder of how much had changed in both their lives. One friend who saw Holiday and Young together before his death stated that both no longer had the fire to perform and to live. After Young's death, life for Holiday had even less meaning than before. She attended the funeral, hoping she would be allowed to sing. But Young's family had little use for his jazz musician friends; Holiday's request was refused. Devastated, Holiday left the church and went to a nearby bar to drown her grief.

A few weeks later, Holiday decided to have a party for her 44th birthday. She invited as many people as she could. She even cooked. As her friends celebrated, Holiday was drinking with alarming speed, causing some concern over her already fragile health. Perhaps she realized that there would not be many more birthdays for her to celebrate. Sick and worn out, Holiday was simply marking time. She struggled through three more dates. Her friends were alarmed over her state of mind and body. She had become almost unrecognizable; she weighed only 95 pounds and was barely strong enough to hold up her head. Still, she found the strength to go on stage and fulfill her obligations, singing the best she could. Her last public appearance came in May 1959 at the Phoenix Theater in Greenwich Village, where she collapsed after two numbers.

On May 30, 1959, Holiday again collapsed in her apartment and was rushed to Knickerbocker Hospital, where she lay comatose for more than an hour before receiving medical attention. She was diagnosed as suffering from acute alcoholism and drug addiction, and Knickerbocker refused her treatment. Transferred to Metropolitan Hospital in Harlem, she again lay on a stretcher unattended. Angered by her treatment, her doctor immediately demanded attention for his patient; soon he had her in a room and under an oxygen tent, where she remained in critical condition. Her doctor later diagnosed Holiday as suffering from cirrhosis and heart failure. Upon hearing the news of Holiday's condition, Louis McKay flew in from the West Coast. Joe Glaser told her doctor not to worry about the hospital bills; he would make sure they were paid.

Even as she lay suffering, Holiday's problems did not go away. Her visitor's list was severely restricted, yet someone was smuggling drugs into her room. Earle Zaidins was also back in the picture, acting as Holiday's spokesman with the media. Behind the scenes, he was trying to get Holiday to leave Joe Glaser for another agency. He took advantage of Holiday's illness to get her to agree to leave Glaser, making sure she signed the contract while she was high on drugs.

On June 11, Holiday's nurse discovered an envelope filled with white powder in her room. Hospital authorities summoned the police, who placed Holiday under arrest and sealed off her hospital room, taking her mug shot and fingerprinting her while she lay in bed. Later, hospital staff said that Holiday could not reach the envelope, as she was hooked up to respiratory equipment. Still, Holiday had round-the-clock police guards, who ordered her flowers, record player, and radio removed from her room. After a series of negotiations with her lawyers, the police agreed that Holiday would not stand trial until she was in better health. She then had to confront Joe Glaser, who learned that she had signed with another agency. Holiday became so distraught over what she had done that she pathetically tried to cancel her new contract by writing a letter asking to be let go. Her new agency never replied.

On July 10, Holiday seemed to be rallying, and her doctors allowed her to receive small gifts of food and candy. Holiday had her hair and nails done and made sure that thank-you notes were written to those who had sent gifts. Then, without warning, she relapsed. Louis McKay never left her side, except to make an early morning phone call on July 17. When he returned to her room, Holiday was dead. She was 44 years old.

The official cause of death was listed as congestion of the lungs compounded by heart failure. What the death certificate did not say was that her condition was brought on by her heavy use of drugs and alcohol or that Holiday was simply worn out.

THE FINAL APPEARANCE

A few days later, more than 10,000 friends, fans, and curiosity seekers went to the Universal Funeral Chapel on Lexington Avenue and 52nd Street, near the area where Holiday's star had shone so brightly for so many years, to pay their last respects. Holiday was laid in an open casket, wearing pink lace. On July 22, 1959, more than 3,000 people attended the funeral mass held at St. Paul's Roman Catholic Church. The church's capacity was 2,100, yet 2,400 managed to squeeze in. Outside the church, hundreds more stood in silent respect. Among those attending the funeral were people who had played some role in the making of the artist known as Billie Holiday, such as Teddy Wilson, John Hammond, Benny Goodman, and a host of musicians who knew "Lady Day."

When the service ended, three limousines and two cars headed to St. Raymond's Cemetery, where Sadie had been laid to rest just a few years before. Before the procession reached the cemetery, it made a slight detour along 110th Street so Harlem could bid farewell to one of its own. At the graveside service, more than 100 people listened to the moving eulogy. Then Holiday's casket was slowly lowered to rest. Fittingly, she was buried beside her mother so that the two would never be apart again. There was solace for some in thinking that her trials were over; that her private hell of addiction, abuse, and pain was at an end. In one of the most moving eulogies of the day, Ralph Gleason stated, "It is sad beyond words that she never knew how many loved her."[7]

A SAD FINALE

When Billie Holiday's body was examined, medical staff found seven hundred fifty dollars taped to her leg: it was literally all the money she had in the world. It turned out that the funds were an advance for a series of autobiographical articles. The fact was Holiday died penniless; what money she had, including the advance, came to only $848.54. She was overdrawn to the tune of more than twenty-five thousand dollars to be paid back on sales of, and royalties from, her records. She owed the Internal Revenue Service more than fourteen hundred dollars in back taxes, and she owed Joe Glaser another eighteen hundred dollars for loans. Her jewelry, cars, and furs had all been sold to pay off debts or to buy drugs. Her estate was so small that it did not qualify for estate taxes.

Even in death, Holiday was not free of her abusers. Earle Zaidins wasted no time in trying to collect more than twelve thousand dollars from Louis McKay that he said was owed him for legal fees. Zaidins told McKay he would drop the claim if he received part of Holiday's estate. McKay agreed, but later had a change of heart. The affair ended up in court, where Zaidins's claim was thrown out. A year after Holiday's death, *Downbeat* magazine reported that McKay had yet to erect a tombstone for his wife. To make things right, the magazine set up a fund to purchase one for Holiday. McKay protested and eventually placed one on her grave. The inscription read:

Beloved wife Billie Holiday known as Lady Day
Born April 7, 1915, Died July 15, 1959.[8]

In a final indignity, McKay had mistaken the date of her death.

NOTES

1. Bud Kliment, *Billie Holiday* (New York: Chelsea House, 1990), p. 90.

2. Julia Blackburn, *With Billie* (New York: Pantheon, 2005), p. 284.

3. Michael Brooks, "Billie Holiday," from *Billie Holiday—The Legacy*, Columbia Jazz Masterpieces, no. 47724, 1991.

4. Stuart Nicholson, *Billie Holiday* (Boston: Northeastern University Press, 1995), p. 197.

5. Ibid., p. 207.

6. Ibid., p. 209.

7. Kliment, *Billie Holiday*, p. 104.

8. Nicholson, *Billie Holiday*, p. 228.

BIBLIOGRAPHY

Baraka, Imiri. *Black Music*. New York: William Morrow, 1968.

"Billie Holiday." Gale-Thompson Free Resources. http://www.gale.com/free_resources/bhm/bio/holiday_b.htm.

Blackburn, Julia. *With Billie*. New York: Pantheon, 2005.

Brooks, Michael. "Billie Holiday." From *Billie Holiday —The Legacy*. Columbia Jazz Masterpieces, no. 47724, 1991.

Burns, Ken. "Race Records." PBS series "Jazz." 2001. http://www.pbs.org/jazz/exchange/exchange_race_records.htm.

Chilton, John. *Billie's Blues*. New York: Stein and Day, 1975.

Clarke, Donald. *Wishing on the Moon: The Life and Times of Billie Holiday*. New York: Viking, 1994.

The Complete Billie Holiday on Verve. 517658–2. Disc 4, track 8.

Daniels, Douglas Henry. *Lester Leaps In: The Life and Times of Lester "Pres" Young*. Boston: Beacon, 2002.

Davis, Angela. *Blues Legacies & Black Feminism: Gertrude "Ma" Rainey, Bessie Smith & Billie Holiday*. New York, Pantheon, 1998.

De Veaux, Alexis. *Don't Explain: A Song of Billie Holiday*. New York: Harper and Row, 1990.

———. *The Billie Holiday Companion: Seven Decades of Commentary*. New York: Schirmer, 1997.

"Earl Hines." World Book.com. http://www.worldbook.com/features/aamusic/html/hines.htm.

Giddins, Gary. *Visions of Jazz: The First Century*. New York: Oxford University Press, 1998.

Gioia, Ted. *The History of Jazz*. New York: Oxford University Press, 1997.

Gourse, Leslie. *Louis' Children: American Jazz Singers*. New York: Quill, 1984.

Hager, Andrew G. *Satin Dolls: The Women of Jazz*. New York: Michael Friedman, 1997.

Hall, Fred. *Dialogues in Swing*. Ventura, CA: Pathfinder, 1989.

Hammond, John, and Irving Townsend. *John Hammond on Record*. London: Penguin, 1981.

Holiday, Billie. Interview. *Ebony*, July 1949.

Holiday, Billie, with William Dufty. *Lady Sings the Blues*. New York: Doubleday, 1956.

James, Burnett. *Billie Holiday*. New York: Hippocrene, 1984.

Jones, Hetty. *Big Star Fallin' Mama: Five Women in Black Music*. New York: Viking, 1997.

Katz, Joel. "Strange Fruit." PBS Independent Lens. http://www.pbs.org/independentlens/strangefruit/film.html.

Kliment, Bud. *Billie Holiday*. New York: Chelsea House, 1990.

Margolick, David. "Strange Fruit." *Vanity Fair*, September 1998. http://www.vanityfair.com/commentary/content/articles/050912roco01a.

———. *Strange Fruit: Billie Holiday, Café Society and the Early Cry for Civil Rights*. Philadelphia: Running Press, 2000.

Montague, Renee. "Artie Shaw: The Reluctant 'King of Swing' Looks Back on Life on the Throne." NPR, March 8, 2002. http://www.npr.org/programs/morning/features/2002/mar/shaw/.

Nicholson, Stuart. *Billie Holiday*. Boston: Northeastern University Press, 1995.

O'Meally, Robert. *Lady Day: The Many Faces of Billie Holiday*. New York: Little, Brown, 1991.

"Review." *New York Age*, December 29, 1934, p. 9.

Shaw, Arnold. *52nd Street: The Street of Jazz*. New York: Da Capo, 1977.

Shaw, Artie. "Journey of Self Discovery." Dave Radlauer JAZZ Rhythm. http://www.jazzhot.bigstep.com/generic5.html.

"Strange Record." *Time*, June 12, 1939. http://www.time.com/time/archive/preview/0,10987,762422,00.html.

"Teddy Wilson." NEA Jazz Masters. http://www.iaje.org/bio.asp? ArtistID = 49.

Vail, Ken. *Lady Day's Diary: The Life of Billie Holiday 1937–1959*. Chessington, UK: Castle Communications, 1996.

White, John. *Billie Holiday*. New York: Universe, 1987.

WEB SITES

Billie Holiday Discography. http://www.billieholiday.be/

The Official Billie Holiday Site. http://www.cmgworldwide.com/music/holiday/

The Unofficial Billie Holiday Web Site. http://www.ladyday.net/
PBS. American Masters: Billie Holiday. http://www.pbs.org/wnet/americanmasters/
    database/holiday_b.html
Jazz Greats: Billie Holiday. http://pbskids.org/jazz/nowthen/billie.html

SELECTED DISCOGRAPHY

Billie Holiday: The Complete Decca Recordings (1944–1950)
The Complete Commodore Recordings (1939–1944)
Lady Day: The Best of Billie Holiday (Columbia, 2001)
Lady Day: The Complete Billie Holiday on Columbia (1933–1944)
Lady in Autumn: The Best of the Verve Years (1946–1959)
Lady in Satin (Columbia, 1958)
Lady Sings the Blues (Verve, 1954–1956)
Love Songs ~ Billie Holiday (Columbia, 1996)
The Ultimate Collection ~ Billie Holiday (Decca, 2005)
The complete Billie Holiday on Verve, 1945–1959
The Commondore Master Takes (1939–1944)
The Quintessential Billie Holiday, Vols. 1–9 (Columbia, 1933–1942)

INDEX

African Americans: allowed atten-
dance at Apollo, 33–34; careers
launched at Apollo, 34; room
accommodation difficulties for, 46
Afro-American Realty Company, 14
Aladdin Recording Company, 99
Albert Hall (London), 101
Allan, Lewis, 68. *See* Meeropol, Abel
Allen, Henry Red, 76
Amsterdam News charity benefit, 85
Apollo Theater: Amateur Night at,
34; Billie's performances at, 66;
Cooper as emcee at, 33
Armstrong, Louis, 26, 29; Billie's
surprise Carnegie Hall appear-
ance with, 88; Wilson's piano
experience with, 36
Arrests: of Billie, 15, 94, 104, 107;
of Florence Williams, 15; of James
Monroe, 75–76; of Sadie Fagan, 15
Ascenido, Jimmy, 89

Baily, Mildred, 21
Baltimore: ghetto neighborhoods of,
1; Holiday (Clarence) returns to,
7; jazz's popularity in, 6
Basie, William "Count": Billie's

touring with, 45–46; Hammond's
interest in, 40, 41–42; relationship
difficulties with Billie, 46–47; and
Swing Era, 48; Young's signing of,
41. *See also* Count Basie Band
"Bebop": birth of, 67; and heroin
usage, 78–79
Berlin, Irving, 68
Billie Holiday Sings album, 99
"Billie's Blues," 37
"Bitter Fruit" poem (Meeropol), 59
Black Swan Records, 29
Blacks: exodus to Harlem, 14; ghetto
neighborhoods of, 1; misery/despair
of, 1; and origins of jazz, 5;
relocation to North by, 5–6
Blake, Eubie, 6
"Body and Soul," 80
Bohny, Lillian, 16
Boogie woogie music, influence of, 66
Boudin, Helen, 7
Bradford, Perry, 27
Bradley, Nita, 50, 51
Bright Spot night club, 19
Brooks, Michael, 101
Brown, James, 34
Brunis, George, 37

Brunswick Records: Billie's recording at studio of, 36–37; Hammond's dealings with, 35

Café Society Band, 61
Café Society club, 55 –57; Billie's final performance at, 66; boogie woogie musicians of, 66; opening of, 67; and "Strange Fruit Grows on Southern Trees," 60
Calloway, Cab, 31
Carnegie Hall (New York City), 55, 87, 88
Carter, Benny, 18–19, 55
Caruso, Enrico, 27
Catagonia Club (Pod and Jerry's), Billie's audition at, 24
"The Chamberlain Crawl" (Meeropol), 57
Chick Webb Orchestra, 35
Clark, Garnett, 24
Clarke, Donald, 15
Clay, Shirley, 30
Clayton, Buck, 46
Club Ebony, 93
Columbia (American) record company, 27; as Billie's first record producer, 28–30; contract expiration from, 75; as Ethel Waters record producer, 28
"Comeback" TV show, 100
Commodore Records, 61
Condon, Eddie, 26
Cooke, Sam, 34
Cooper, Ralph: as bandleader in Harlem, 33; with his 18 Kings of Melody, 34
Cotton Club, 15
Count Basie Band, struggles of, 44
Covan's night club, 20, 23

Dance crazes, 15
Death: of Billie, 107; of Clarence Holiday, 43–44; of Lester Young, 106; of Sadie Fagan, 82, 85

Decca Records, 79, 86
Dietrich, Marlene, 29
Dixon, Martha "Mattie," 2
Dorsey, Jimmy, 37
Dorsey Brothers, and Swing Era, 48
Dougherty, Eddie, 61
Dove, Billie, 16
Downbeat club (New York City), 80–81
Downbeat magazine, 50, 77; Billie's popularity poll rankings in, 88; praise by, 102
Drinking/drug usage: by Billie, 19, 81; financial costs of, 85, 98; in hospital, 107; and jazz musicians, 78–79; temperament influenced by, 25–26
Dufty, William, 102–3
Duncan, Laura, 59

Ed Fishman Agency, 91
Ed Small's Paradise, 18
El Dumpo club (Chicago), 56
Eldridge, Roy, 55
Ellington, Duke, 15, 31, 48
Ellis, Ray, 105–6
Esquire Magazine Jazz Concert, 80
Europe, Billie's tour of, 100–102

Fagan, Charles: Catholic conversion by, 2; as father of Sara (Harris), 2
Fagan, Sadie (aka Sara Harris; Billie's mother): arrest of, 15; churchgoing activities of, 8; death of, 82, 85; as employee of Williams, 13; entrepreneurial ventures of, 8; financial difficulties of, 7–8; Gough's marriage to/abandonment of, 8; and influence of Clarence Holiday's death, 44; return to Baltimore by, 7
Fairbanks, Douglas, 16
Famous Door club, 37, 72
FBI, and Billie, 69
Fishman, Edward, lawsuit v. Billie by, 97
Fitzgerald, Ella, 34; Billie's curiosity about, 35

Forest, Helen, 51
Foster, Pop, on Billie's drug usage/
  drinking, 25–26
Fowler, Billy, 7
Fox, Ed, 38
Freddie Kreppard and his Original
  Creole Orchestra, 27

Gabler, Milt, 61; Decca recording
  contract arranged by, 79; toler-
  ance for Billie's drinking/drug
  usage, 86
Garland, Judy, 31
Gaye, Marvin, 34
Gershwin, Ira, 57
Gilford, Jack, 56
Glaser, Joe, 26; Billie's business
  association with, 38; management
  by, 75, 99; ultimatum by, 89
Glover, Ruby, 6
"God Bless the Child," 77
Goodman, Benny: African American
  musicians employed by, 26,
  67; Billie's recordings with, 29;
  Brunswick studio sessions, 36–37;
  and Swing Era, 48; Wilson's
  experience playing with, 36
Gordon, Robert, 59
Gough, Philip, abandonment by, 8
Grand Terrace Ballroom, 38, 79
Granz, Norman, 99
Great Depression, 17–18
Guthrie, Woody, 87
Guy, Joseph Luke, 80, 81

Hammond, John: Basie's viewing
  by, 40, 41–42; as Billie's unofficial
  press agent, 26; collaboration
  with, 21; as fan of Billie, 20–21;
  and Josephson, 56; Mills' employment of, 31; *Spirituals To Sing*
  concert of, 55; as writer for *Melody
  Maker,* 20; writings about Billie
  by, 23, 30
Hanighen, Bernie, 26

Harlem (New York City): and Black
  exodus from South, 14; Catagonia Club of, 24; Cotton Club
  of, 15; ethnic makeup of, 14;
  Hammond's performances in, 20;
  as Negro capital of world, 13–14;
  Renaissance of, 29
Harlem Stride, 14–15
Harris, Eleanora (aka Billie
  Holiday): arrest of, 15; Good
  Shepherd problems of, 8; lesbian-
  ism introduction of, 8; Moore as
  role model for, 9; name change to
  "Billie " by, 16; parental concerns
  of young, 7; as self-sufficient young
  girl, 9; singing as love/aspiration of,
  9–10, 15; as young prostitute, 13
Harris, Sara (aka Sadie Fagan):
  Catholic conversion by, 2;
  Eleanora's birth by, 3; Holiday
  (Clarence) seduction of, 2; humble
  origins of, 2; pregnancy of, 2–3. *See
  also* Fagan, Sadie
Hawkins, Coleman, 41, 45
Henderson, Bobby: Apollo Theater
  invitation for, 30; Billie's clash
  with, 24–25; engagement/broken
  engagement with Billie, 25
Henderson, Fletcher, 7, 15; Billie's
  clash with, 38; Holliday (Clarence)
  as guitarist with, 19–20; Young's
  playing with, 41
Heroin addiction. *See* Drinking/drug
  usage
Hill, Wee Wee, 8–9
Hines, Earl "Fatha," 36
Hippodrome club (New York City), 66
Hironimus, Helen, 91
Hitler, Adolph, 57
Holiday, Billie: Apollo Theater
  invitation for, 30; arrests of, 15.94,
  94, 104, 107; automobile accident
  of, 76; bad side/temper/stubborn-
  ness of, 25; as "Best Vocalist,"
  80; bisexuality/lesbianism of, 8,

66; and Café Society, 57, 66; and
Clarence Holiday's death, 43–44;
comeback concert of, 92–93;
"Comeback" tv appearance by,
100; death of, 107; Decca Record's
signing of, 79, 86; drinking/drug
usage, 19, 25–26, 81; Ed Fishman Agency management of, 91;
elusive/enigmatic qualities of, 1;
enduring musical influence of, 45;
engagement/broken engagement
with Henderson (Bobby), 25; European tour by, 100–102; FBI's files
on, 69; final years of, 103–5; first
recording attempt by, 28–30; Glaser, Joe: business association with,
38; management by, 26; ultimatum
by, 89; Good Shepherd problems
of, 8; Goodman's recordings with,
29; Hammond's collaboration
with, 21; Hironimus' friendship
of, 91–92; "Holiday on Broadway"
revue performance by, 93; incarceration of, 90–92; "Lady Day"
nickname of, 17; "Lady" nickname
of, 44; "Lady Yester-Day" nickname of, 103; life's downturn for,
78–79; and love of saxophone,
16; majesty/regalness of, 67–68;
masochistic nature of, 77, 94; microphone anxiety of, 29; missteps
by, 37–39; Monroe's marriage to,
70–72; Moore as role model for, 9;
musical choices made by, 45–46,
49–50; new sophisticated look of,
40; parental concerns of young,
7; racism problems of, 50–51;
recording career success of, 39–40;
relationship difficulties with Basie,
46–47; relationship/marriage with
McKay, 98–99, 104; and Sadie's
death, 85; as self-sufficient young
girl, 9; Shaw's association with,
48–49; signature style of, 30, 34;

singing as love/aspiration of, 9–10,
15; Smith's replacement of, 38;
standards of, 17; "Strange Fruit
Grows on Southern Trees": legacy
of, 62–64; positive influence on career, 65; touring with Basie, 45–46;
as an "up" girl, 17; venues played
by, 66; as waitress at Mexico's restaurant, 18, 23–34; white gardenia
trademark of, 66–67; Wilson's arrangements for, 36; as young prostitute, 13; and Young's death, 106;
Young's deep friendship with, 42,
44–45. See also Harris, Eleanora
Holiday, Clarence (Billie's father):
army enlistment of, 6; band
travels by, 7; Billie's relationship
with, 19–20; death of, 43–44;
Harris (Sara) seduced by, 2;
marriage to Helen Boudin, by,
7; Miller home visited by, 7; as
young guitarist, 6
Holiday, Fanny (Clarence's third
wife), 44
"Holiday on Broadway" revue, 93
Holliday, Nelson (father of
Clarence), 6
Holton, Kenneth, 16, 61
"Home of the Happy Feet." See Savoy
Ballroom
Horne, Lena, 34
Hot-Cha club, 30, 34; Billie's return
to, 35
Hotel Sherman, radio broadcasts
from, 68
House of Good Shepherd for Colored
Girls, 8

"I Cried for You," 37, 77
"I Must Have that Man," 37
"If the Moon Turns Green"
(Hanighen), 26
Incarceration: of Billie, 90–92; of
Monroe, 76

Jazz: in Baltimore, 6; *modernism's* influence on, 5; origins of, 3–6; and racial animosity/violence, 3–4
Jazz Club USA European shows, 101
Jeffries, Herb, 35
Joe Sherman Garrick Stagebar, 76
Johnson, Charlie, 18
Johnson, James P., 14
Johnson, Marge, Billie's discovery by, 18
Johnston, Mary (mother of Clarence Holliday), 6
Jordan, Louis, 34
Josephson, Barney, and Café Society club, 55 –57

Kelly's Stable club, 67
Keppard, Freddie, 27
Kings of Melody. *See* Ralph Cooper with his 18 Kings of Melody
Knight, Richard, on origins of jazz, 4
Kongo Knights band, 33

"Lady Day," as nickname of Billie, 17
Lady in Satin album, 105–6
"Lady," nickname of Billie, 44
Lady Sings the Blues autobiography (Holiday, Billie), 7, 102
"Lady Yester-Day," as nickname of Billie, 103
Levy, John, 93; Billie's leaving of, 97; drug setup attempt by, 94; financial mismanagement by, 94
Lincoln Hotel (New York City), 51–52
"Long Gone Blues," 37, 66
"Lover Man," 80
Lynchings, 57–59

"The Man I Love," 37
Markham, Pigmeat, 35
Matthews, Emmett, 34
McCarthy, Joseph, 88

McKay, Louis: Billie's drug-related marriage to, 104; Billie's relationship with, 98–99
McKinley Gardens (Brooklyn) concert, 87
McKinley Theater (New York City), 81
McKinney's Cotton Pickers, 7
McLin, Jimmy, 61
Meeropol, Abel: "Bitter Fruit" poem of, 59; lynching's impact on, 59; and Rosenberg sons, 57
Melody Maker, 20, 26
Mercer, Johnny, 29
Mexico's restaurant: Billie's employment at, 18, 23–34; meeting Hanighen at, 26
Miller, Eva (Sadie's half-sister), 3
Miller, Glenn, and Swing Era, 48
Miller, Robert, 3
Mills, Irving, 31
Monroe, Clarke, 43
Monroe, James: Billie's love affair with, 68; Billie's marriage to, 70–72; drug smuggling arrest of, 75–76; incarceration of, 76; Uptown House visits by, 70
Moore, Ethel: as role model for Eleanora, 9; Wilson as piano accompanist to, 20
"More Than You Know," 55
Musicians. *See* Allen, Henry Red; Armstrong, Louis; Basie, William "Count"; Cooper, Ralph; Dougherty, Eddie; Eldridge, Roy; Ellington, Duke; Goodman, Benny; Guy, Joseph Luke; Hawkins, Coleman; Hines, Earl "Fatha"; Holton, Kenneth; McLin, Jimmy; Mercer, Johnny; Miller, Glenn; Newton, Frankie; Parker, Charlie; Payne, Stan; Peterson, Oscar; Shaw, Artie; Shearing, George; Simmons, John; Tucker,

Bobby; Waller, Fats; White, Sonny; Williams, John; Wilson, Garland; Wilson, Teddy; Young, Lester

National Association for the Advancement of Colored People (NAACP), 62
Nest Club, 16
New Orleans: and birth of jazz, 3, 5; racial diversity of, 5
New Orleans movie: and McCarthyism, 88; soundtrack recording for, 87–88
New York Age magazine, 25, 30
New York City: American Columbia studio in, 28; Billie's arrival in, 13; Carnegie Hall of, 55, 87, 88; Famous Door club of, 37; Hippodrome club of, 66; Lincoln Hotel of, 51–52; McKinley Theater of, 81; Onyx Club of, 39; Phoenix Theater of, 106; "the Street" of, 66–67; Town Hall of, 87; Uptown House of, 66. *See also* Harlem (New York City)
New York Teacher union publication, 59
Newport Jazz Festival (1954), 102
Newton, Frankie, 56, 61
Nicholson, Stuart, 59–60
Nicknames, of Billie Holiday: "Lady," 44; "Lady Day," 17; "Lady Yester-Day," 103
Night clubs: Bright Spot, 19; Café Society, 55 –57; Catagonia Club, 24; Club Ebony, 93; Covan's, 20; Downbeat, 80–81; El Dumpo, 56; Famous Door, 37, 72; Grand Terrace Ballroom, 38, 79; Hippodrome, 66; Hot-Cha, 30; Joe Sherman Garrick Stagebar, 76; Kelly's Stable, 67; Onyx Club, 39, 40, 77, 89; Reno Club, 40; Spotlite (New York City), 80; Stork Club,

56; Sunset, 30; Troutville Club, 76; Uptown House, 66
Norvo, Red, 21, 101

O'Day, Anita, 97
Okeh record company, 27
Onyx Club: Billie's return to, 77, 89; hiring-firing-rehiring of Billie at, 39, 40
Original Dixieland Jazz Band, 27
"Over Here, the Yanks Aren't Coming," 68

Palomar Ballroom (Los Angeles), 48
Paramount record company, 27
Parker, Charlie, 45
Paul Whiteman Orchestra, 76
Payne, Stan, 61
Payton, Phillip A., 14
Peterson, Oscar, 102
Phoenix Theater (New York City), 106
Piaf, Édith, 29
Plessy v. Ferguson Supreme Court decision, 4
Pod and Jerry's. *See* Catagonia Club
Preston, Jerry, 24
Prostitution, Gough's beginnings in, 13

"Race records," 27
Racism: and birth of jazz, 3–4; and death of Clarence Holiday, 42; and lynchings, 57–58; and *Plessy v. Ferguson* decision, 4; and shame of United States, 58; and Shaw, 50; towards Billie, 50–51
Ralph Cooper with his 18 Kings of Melody, 34, 35
RCA Victor Talking Machine Company, 27
Record companies, 27, 79, 86
"A Red Under My Bed" (Meeropol), 57
Redmon, Don, 7

Reno Club, 40
"Riffin' the Scotch," 29, 30
Rockwell-O'Keefe Agency, 38
Royal Theater (Baltimore), 81

"Saddest Tale," 31
Savoy Ballroom, 15
Seeger, Pete, 87
Shaw, Artie: Billie's association with,
    48–49; Billie's walking out on,
    52; and racism problems, 50; and
    Swing Era, 48
Shearing, George, 102
Simmons, John, 77
Sinatra, Frank, 31
Singing, Billie's love/aspirations of,
    9–10, 15
Smith, Bessie, 29, 38
Smith, Clay, 3
Smith, Stuff, 39
Smith, Tab, 61
Smith, Willie "the Lion," 14, 24; on
    Billie's drinking/drug usage, 26
Snowden, Elmer, 6
"Some Other Spring," 66
Songs, sung by Billie Holiday: Billie
    Holiday Sings album, 99; "Billie's
    Blues," 37; "Body and Soul," 80;
    "God Bless the Child," 77; "He
    Ain't Got Rhythm," 42; "I Cried
    for You," 37, 77; "I Must Have That
    Man," 37, 42; "Long Gone Blues,"
    37, 66; "Lover Man," 80; "The
    Man I Love," 37; "More Than You
    Know," 55; "Over Here, the Yanks
    Aren't Coming," 68; "Some Other
    Spring," 66; "Strange Fruit Grows
    on Southern Trees," 59–62; "Them
    There Eyes," 37, 66; "This Year's
    Kisses," 42; "When a Woman Loves
    a Man," 26; "Why Was I Born," 42;
    "Wouldja for a Big Red Apple"?,
    21; "You Let Me Down," 38
Sousa, John Phillip, 27

South, Black exodus from, 14
Speakeasies, of Prohibition era, 67
Spirituals To Sing concert (of
    Hammond), 55
Spotlite club (New York City), 80
Statue, of Billy Holiday, 1
Stork Club, 56
Strand Theater, 93
"Strange Fruit Grows on Southern
    Trees," 59–60; as "Best Song of
    Twentieth Century," 64; impact/
    recording of, 61–62; legacy of,
    62–64; positive influence on
    Billie's career, 65; success of, 62;
    Time magazine on, 64; Variety
    magazine on, 60
Stuff Smith and his Sextet, 39
Sunset club, 30
"Sweet Mama Stringbean," as nick-
    name of Ethel Waters, 29
Swing Era (1935-1946), 48
Symphony in Black film, 31

Teagarden, Charles, 30
"The Street," clubs and restaurants
    of, 66–67
"Them There Eyes," 37, 66
Time magazine, 64
Torch singers, 29
Town Hall (New York City), 87
Trademark, white gardenia, of Billie,
    66–67
Troutville Club (L.A.), 76
Tucker, Bobby, 89

United States, racist shame of, 58
"Up" girls, 17
Uptown House (New York City),
    66, 70

Vanderbilt, William Henry, 20
Variety magazine, 60
Victor Talking Machine
    Company, 27

Victrola record player, 27
Vocalion record company, 27

Waller, Fats, 14
Waters, Ethel, 28, 29; as Sweet Mama Stringbean, 29
Watkins, Ralph, 68
Webb, Chick, 6, 15, 35
Weill, Kurt, 57
"When a Woman Loves a Man" (Hanighen), 26
White, Sonny, 61
White gardenia trademark, of Billie, 66–67
Whiteman, Paul, 76
"Who Loves You," 37
Wilde, Al, 93
Williams, Florence: arrest of, 15; as Harlem madam, 13
Williams, John, 61

Wilson, Garland (pianist), 20
Wilson, Teddy, 35, 37, 55; Billie's arrangements by, 36; Newport Jazz Festival appearance, 102; playing experience with Armstrong, 36
Wishing on the Moon (Clarke), 15
"Wouldja for a Big Red Apple?" song, 21
Wright, Marcus, 30

"You Let Me Down," 38
Young, Lester, 4, 40–41; Billie's deep friendship with, 42, 44–45; death of, 106; enduring musical influence of, 45; "Pres" as nickname of, 44
Young, Trummy, 76
"Your Mother's Son-in-Law," 29, 30

Zaidins, Earle Warren, 104
Ziegfeld Follies, 16

ABOUT THE AUTHOR

MEG GREENE is an independent scholar and prolific biographer. She is the author of biographies on Jane Goodall, Mother Teresa, and Pope John Paul II for Greenwood Press.